# Quick and Easy Math

## FOR GRADES 3-6

## Tina Thoburn, Ed.D. and Terry Kane

**Troll Associates**

**Interior Illustrations by Shirley Beckes**

ISBN: 0-8167-3273-6
Printed in the United States of America
10 9 8 7 6 5 4 3 2 1

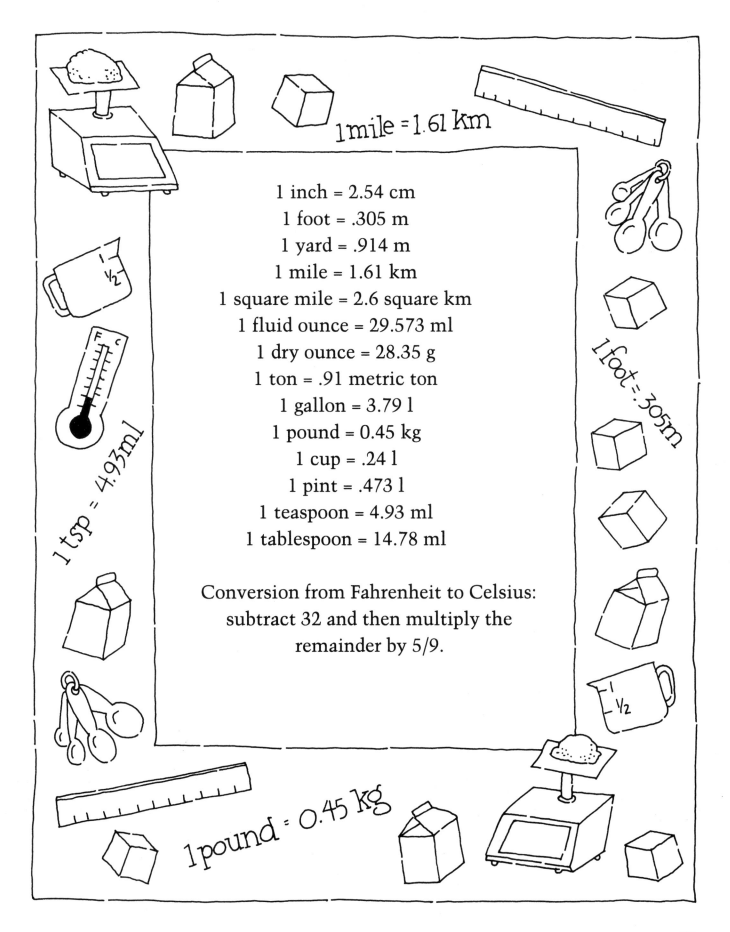

1 inch = 2.54 cm
1 foot = .305 m
1 yard = .914 m
1 mile = 1.61 km
1 square mile = 2.6 square km
1 fluid ounce = 29.573 ml
1 dry ounce = 28.35 g
1 ton = .91 metric ton
1 gallon = 3.79 l
1 pound = 0.45 kg
1 cup = .24 l
1 pint = .473 l
1 teaspoon = 4.93 ml
1 tablespoon = 14.78 ml

Conversion from Fahrenheit to Celsius:
subtract 32 and then multiply the
remainder by 5/9.

# •CONTENTS•

# •INTRODUCTION•

Have you been searching for new math games and activities to provide students with enjoyable math experiences? *Quick and Easy Math for Grades 3-6* to the rescue! Here you will find a variety of puzzles, games, reproducibles, and manipulative activities to help children understand numbers, geometry, and measurement, as well as build skills in logic, critical thinking, and problem solving.

One of the main objectives of math instruction in the upper elementary grades is to strengthen students' number sense. In order to work productively with numbers in the real world, students need to understand what whole numbers are, how they are represented in place value notation, and how they compare with each other. Students in grades 3-6 should be alert to number patterns and grasp how numbers behave under operations such as multiplication and division. Many theme-based activities in *Quick and Easy Math for Grades 3-6* focus on these topics.

Next, explorations with fractions and decimals extend students' understanding of numbers. Imaginative activities teach them to compare, order, and add and subtract fractions and decimals.

Children encounter many examples of geometry in the real world. With *Quick and Easy Math for Grades 3-6*, they'll enjoy identifying three-dimensional shapes and creating their own tangram designs.

Measurement concepts are best developed over time through concrete experiences. The activities in this book provide hands-on familiarity with perimeter, area, and volume. Students use standard or metric units of length and area as well as imaginary outer-space units of volume.

Time and money activities are related both to everyday events and fictional situations. Students calculate elapsed time and use schedules to solve problems. They count and compare money—then add, subtract, multiply, and divide it.

Today's math educators want children to learn to solve problems and think logically and critically. While all the activities involve these critical skills, the last section of *Quick and Easy Math for Grades 3-6* addresses logic most directly. Students are challenged to examine information from diverse sources and reach satisfactory solutions.

Cooperative learning is a key ingredient of each activity in *Quick and Easy Math for Grades 3-6*. Student groups provide a safe, supportive, fun atmosphere in which to practice new math skills. Children help each other manipulate concrete materials, illustrate their findings, and engage in healthy debate as they learn deeper mathematical concepts.

## •HOW TO USE THIS BOOK•

Each lesson in *Quick and Easy Math for Grades 3-6* begins with several hands-on math activities designed to show a particular math concept in action. After you demonstrate the activity, invite volunteers to demonstrate them as well. Make available ample copies of the manipulative reproducibles, such as the game boards, fraction strips, and tangram patterns, so that students can try them out frequently with each other.

After students practice the hands-on math activities, they will be all set to complete the reproducible sheets individually. Wind up each lesson by encouraging students to share their answers and their methods for reaching them.

With these versatile approaches and activities, *Quick and Easy Math for Grades 3-6* reinforces students' math concepts while helping them to experience math in brand-new ways.

# Odd Enough?

**Objective: Understanding odd and even numbers**

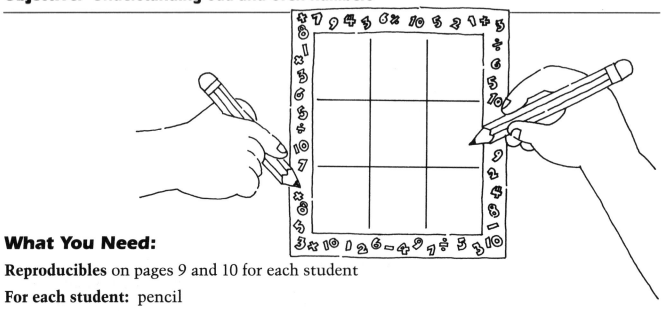

## What You Need:

**Reproducibles** on pages 9 and 10 for each student

**For each student:** pencil

**For sharing:** blocks

## What You Do:

**1.** Ask students if they can tell if a number is odd or even. If not, write the numbers one through ten on the chalkboard. Circle the even numbers and underline the odd numbers. Ask for volunteers to stack blocks in two piles, one odd and one even. Point out that the uneven pile is made up of an odd number of blocks. The even pile can be divided equally in half.

**2.** If students already know even and odd numbers, you can explain that even numbers always can be divided into groups of twos with none left over. Point out that the sum of two even numbers is always even, that the sum of two odd numbers is always even, and the sum of an odd number and an even number is always odd.

**3.** Show the class how to play a variation of "Tic-Tac-Toe." Hand out the **reproducible** on page 9 to pairs of students. Explain that one player enters only even numbers in the grid, while the other enters only odd numbers. The first player to enter a number that makes a row up, down, or diagonally add up to fifteen wins the round.

**4.** Distribute the **reproducible** on page 10. Read the directions aloud and let the students solve the maze on their own.

Answer for page 10: Door #3

**8**

# Tic-Tac-Toe

Name_____ Date_____

# Wizard's Walk

Which door hides the magic potion?  Add or subtract the problems.  Then color the odd-numbered answers to help the wizard find the path to the correct door.

| | | | |
|---|---|---|---|
| 32 +58 | 97 −31 | 43 +25 | 86 −22 |
| 89 −52 | 27 + 6 | 71 −48 | 36 +35 | 82 −57 |
| 50 −28 | 62 +36 | 75 −41 | 51 +13 | 94 −23 |
| 67 −33 | 17 +61 | 43 +28 | 75 −34 | 15 +48 |
| 77 −35 | 42 +18 | 70 −23 | 12 +54 | 21 −19 |

# Great, Greater, Greatest!

**Objective: Understanding place value of large numbers**

## What You Need:

**Reproducible** on page 12 for each student

**For each student:** pencil and three slips of paper; three boxes (tissue boxes or shoe boxes work well)

## What You Do:

**1.** Show students a very simple way to compare numbers. Write two five-digit numbers on the chalkboard, vertically aligning the digits. Explain that they can compare the numbers by looking at the digits at the far left. If those are the same, they should then compare the digits second from the left, and so on. When they see different digits in the same place value column, they should check which digit is greater.

**2.** To help students practice this skill, write two ten-digit numbers on the board. Ask a volunteer to show which number is greater. Repeat the exercise until everyone has had a chance to compare numbers.

**3.** Review the symbols for "equals," "is greater than," and "is less than" with the children. To assess understanding, ask volunteers to work at the chalkboard. Give each child two Heavy Hippo names from the **reproducible** on page 12 and ask them to compare the hippos' weights using the proper symbols.

**4.** Give each student three small slips of paper. Ask them to write any three-digit number on each slip. Then reveal three boxes labeled "< 850," "> 250," and "Between 250 and 850." (You can choose any range of numbers you like.) Have students put their slips in the correct boxes. Small groups of students can check the numbers.

**5.** Distribute the **reproducible** on page 12 to each child. Read the directions aloud before students work on the sheets independently.

Answers for page 12: 1. 4,096 < 4,275; 2. 4,391 > 3,916; 3. 3,910 > 3,827; 4. 4,391 > 4,096

Name_____ Date_____

# Heavyweight Hippos

All the hippos are getting weighed today.  Can you figure out which hippo is a heavyweight?

Hubble        Hildoodle        Homeree

Hinky        Hulda        Hizzy

**1.** Compare Homeree's weight and Hulda's weight. _____

**2.** Compare Hubble's weight and Hildoodle's weight. _____

**3.** Compare Hinky's weight and Hizzy's weight. _____

**4.** Compare Hubble's weight and Homeree's weight. _____

Answers on page 11

# Faster Than You Can Count!

**Objective:  Understanding basic multiplication facts**

## What You Need:

**Reproducible** on page 14 for each student

**For sharing:**  counters; set of dominoes (to nines)

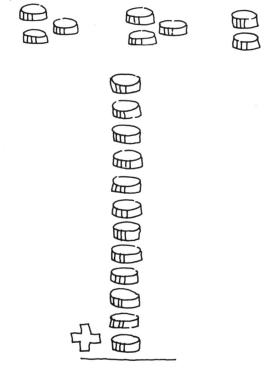

## What You Do:

**1.** Remind students that multiplication is like addition but usually much faster. Demonstrate how to use counters (or buttons, paper clips, etc.) to model the multiplication facts.  To show 4 x 3, place four groups of three counters on the table.  Then push the groups together and count the counters for a sum of twelve.  Demonstrate a few more facts, inviting volunteers to try it, too.  Keep counters available at all times for students to use if they forget a fact or just want to check their work.

**2.** Place a set of dominoes (up to nines) face down on the table.  Divide the class into two teams.  One student from each team takes turns picking a domino from the table and telling the product of the two numbers on the domino.  A correct product earns one point. The first team to score twenty-five points wins.

**3.** Distribute the **reproducible** on page 14. Read the directions aloud before the students work individually on the sheets.  Allow students to use the counters to work out any difficult problems.

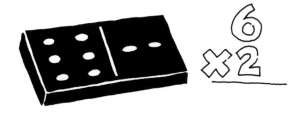

Answers for page 14: helmets: 16, 10, 21;  eye protectors: 16, 40, 42; shoes: 24, 40, 28;  gloves: 20, 20, 49;  earrings: 64, 20, 126

Name_____ Date_____

# Heads Up

Gylipshix is in charge of uniforms for the space team. How many of each item should he order?

|  | The Space Team | | |
|---|---|---|---|
| | **One Gleep has:** | **One Nerphed has:** | **One Ominum has:** |
| | 4 heads | 2 heads | 3 heads |
| | 1 eye per head | 4 eyes per head | 2 eyes per head |
| | 6 feet | 8 feet | 4 feet |
| | 5 hands | 4 hands | 7 hands |
| | 4 ears per head | 2 ears per head | 6 ears per head |
| | 4 Gleeps | 5 Nerpheds | 7 Ominums |
| **helmets** | | | |
| **eye protectors** | | | |
| **shoes** | | | |
| **gloves** | | | |
| **earrings** | | | |

Answers on page 13

# Double Trouble

**Objective:** Understanding multiplication of two-digit numbers by a one-digit number

4 GROUPS OF 10 ONES BLOCKS

4 TENS BLOCKS

## What You Need:

**Reproducible** on page 16 for each student

**For sharing:** tens and ones place-value blocks; number cubes, numbered one through six

## What You Do:

**1.** Quickly review the concept of multiplication as putting sets of the same size together. Use tens place-value blocks to model the problem 4 x 10. You might remind students that multiplying a number in the tens place is just like multiplying a number in the ones place. Write the problem and the product on the chalkboard. Model another problem, such as 5 x 23, which requires regrouping. Remind students to trade ten ones blocks for a ten block whenever possible.

**2.** Group students into pairs. Then write five two-digit numbers on the chalkboard in one column and two one-digit numbers in another column. One partner selects a one-digit number, and the other selects a two-digit number. The partners work together to find the product of the numbers. They can use the place-value blocks to model their problems.

**3.** Group the class into two teams standing in two lines facing the chalkboard. After you call out a multiplication problem, each student standing first in each line races to the board, writes the product, and returns to the end of the line. The first correct answer scores one point for the team. The next in each line is challenged with a new problem. The first team to earn twenty points wins.

**4.** Give each student the **reproducible** on page 16. Review the directions with the class before students complete the sheets on their own. Let students use place-value blocks to check their work.

Answers for page 16: Tree 1=102 leaves; Tree 2 =128 leaves; Tree 3 = 135 leaves; Tree 4=245 leaves;
Tree 5=171 leaves; Tree 6 =138 leaves
1. Tree 4; 2. Tree 2; 3. Tree 3; 4. Tree 1; 5. Tree 5; 6. Tree 6

Name_____Date_____

# Feeding Times

Each giraffe needs to eat a certain number of leaves. Write the number of leaves on the line below each tree. Then write the number of the tree that has the nearest number of leaves to feed each giraffe what it needs.

**Tree 1**
17 leaves
per branch
6 branches
_____

**Tree 2**
32 leaves
per branch
4 branches
_____

**Tree 3**
27 leaves
per branch
5 branches
_____

**Tree 4**
35 leaves
per branch
7 branches
_____

**Tree 5**
19 leaves
per branch
9 branches
_____

**Tree 6**
46 leaves
per branch
3 branches
_____

**1.** Gert eats 209 leaves.

Tree: ___

**2.** Geff eats 122 leaves.

Tree: ___

**3.** Gonny eats 134 leaves.

Tree: ___

**4.** Gerry eats 98 leaves.

Tree: ___

**5.** Gim eats 164 leaves.

Tree: ___

**6.** Galph eats 136 leaves.

Tree: ___

# More Multiplication

**Objective: Understanding multiplication of three-digit numbers by one-digit numbers**

## What You Need:

**Reproducible** on page 18 for each child

**For sharing:** an assortment of hundreds, tens, and ones place-value blocks; four number cubes of any denomination

## What You Do:

**1.** Quickly review multiplying a two-digit number by a one-digit number. Use place-value blocks to demonstrate that sets of the same size go together. Pose a problem that involves multiplying a three-digit number by a one-digit number, such as 352 x 4. Ask a volunteer to model the problem using the place-value blocks. Repeat this activity until everyone has had a turn modeling a problem.

**2.** Divide the class into two teams. One team tosses the four number cubes and makes a "one-digit times three-digit" multiplication problem. The other team solves the problem. A correct answer earns that team points equal to the number of regroupings necessary in the problem. For example, if the number cubes turned up 4, 9, 2, 6, the problem would be: 492 x 6 = 2,952. There are three regroupings required to solve this problem, so the team gets three points. The first team to earn twenty points is the winner.

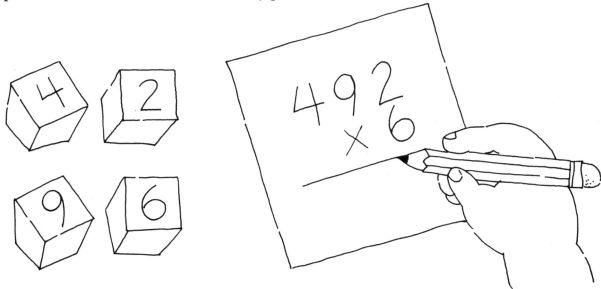

**3.** Distribute the **reproducible** on page 18 to each student. Read the directions aloud before students complete the sheets individually.

Answers for page 18: 2,380 steaks; 5,915 cans of peanuts; 3,346 spareribs; 3,675 popcorn balls; 8,575 bales of hay; 5,544 bananas

Name_____ Date_____

# Creature Feature

Klem is in charge of feeding the animals at the zoo. Find out how much of each food he should order for next week (Monday through Sunday). Then fill out the order blank.

| Animal | Food Per Day | Animal | Food Per Day |
|--------|--------------|--------|--------------|
| **Lions** | 142 steaks<br>265 spareribs | **Antelope** | 328 bales of hay<br>112 popcorn balls |
| **Tigers** | 213 spareribs<br>198 steaks | **Elephant** | 622 bales of hay<br>548 cans of peanuts |
| **Yaks** | 275 bales of hay<br>413 popcorn balls | **Monkeys** | 792 bananas<br>297 cans of peanuts |

**Order Form**

_____ steaks        _____ cans of peanuts

_____ spareribs     _____ popcorn balls

_____ bales of hay  _____ bananas

# Divide and Conquer

**Objective: Understanding division by one through five**

## What You Need:

**Reproducibles** on pages 20 and 21-22 for
groups of three to four students each

**For sharing:** baking cups; counters;
fact cards for multiplication and
division (to five)

## What You Do:

**1.** Explain the idea of division to the class.
Point out that when you divide, you are
making equal smaller sets from one larger
set. Ask students to explain how division compares to multiplication. (It is the opposite.
In multiplication, you are putting smaller sets together. In division, you are breaking a
large set into smaller ones.)

**2.** Use baking cups and counters (or buttons or dried beans) to model division facts for the
class. Write a division fact on the chalkboard, such as $12 \div 4$. Count out twelve counters and
place them on the table. Count out four cups and place them on the table. Take the counters
and put one in each cup. Repeat this until the counters are gone. Ask how many counters are
in each cup (3). Write the dividend to the division fact on the board. Write several more division facts on the board and have students work in pairs or small groups to model the facts.

**3.** Use fact cards to show students a multiplication and division fact family. Have them
explain why we think of these four facts as a "family." (They use the same numbers.) Mix
the cards well and distribute them all to the children and yourself. Select one of your cards
and show it to the class. Those students who have the other members of that fact family
should bring their cards to the front of the room, where the entire "family" can be displayed.

**4.** Organize students into groups of three or four, giving each group a pair of scissors and the
**reproducibles** on pages 21 and 22. Allow time to cut apart the flower sheet. Explain that the
groups will have to figure out how to divide the flowers so that the ogres on page 20 each get
an equal number of their favorite flowers.

Answers for page 20:

|    | roses | irises | lilies | petunias | daisies |
|----|-------|--------|--------|----------|---------|
| 1. | 5     | 3      | 2      | 4        | 0       |
| 2. | 5     | 3      | 2      | 0        | 0       |
| 3. | 5     | 3      | 0      | 0        | 0       |
| 4. | 5     | 0      | 0      | 0        | 0       |
| 5. | 5     | 3      | 2      | 4        | 4       |
| 6. | 0     | 0      | 0      | 0        | 0       |

Name_____ Date_____

# Bouquets for Ogres

These ogres like different flowers.  Count how many ogres like each kind of flower.
Then divide to find how many of each flower they should get.

Likes roses, petunias,
lilies, and irises

Likes roses
and lilies and irises

Likes roses and irises

Likes roses

Likes roses, irises, petunias,
lilies, and daisies

Doesn't like anything

You have 25 roses, 12 irises, 6 lilies, 8 petunias, and 4 daisies.
Give the flowers to those ogres who like them.

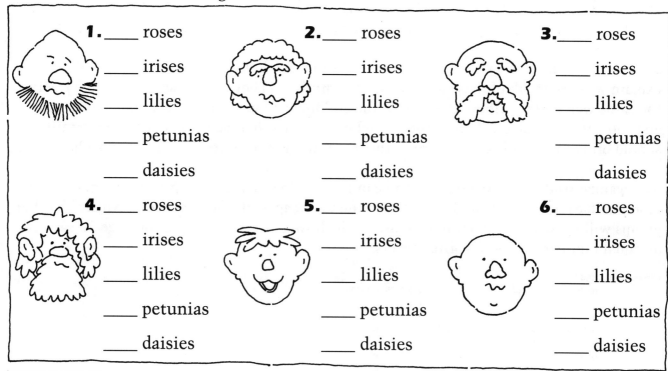

**1.** ____ roses
____ irises
____ lilies
____ petunias
____ daisies

**2.** ____ roses
____ irises
____ lilies
____ petunias
____ daisies

**3.** ____ roses
____ irises
____ lilies
____ petunias
____ daisies

**4.** ____ roses
____ irises
____ lilies
____ petunias
____ daisies

**5.** ____ roses
____ irises
____ lilies
____ petunias
____ daisies

**6.** ____ roses
____ irises
____ lilies
____ petunias
____ daisies

Answers on page 19

# Ogres' Flower Sheet

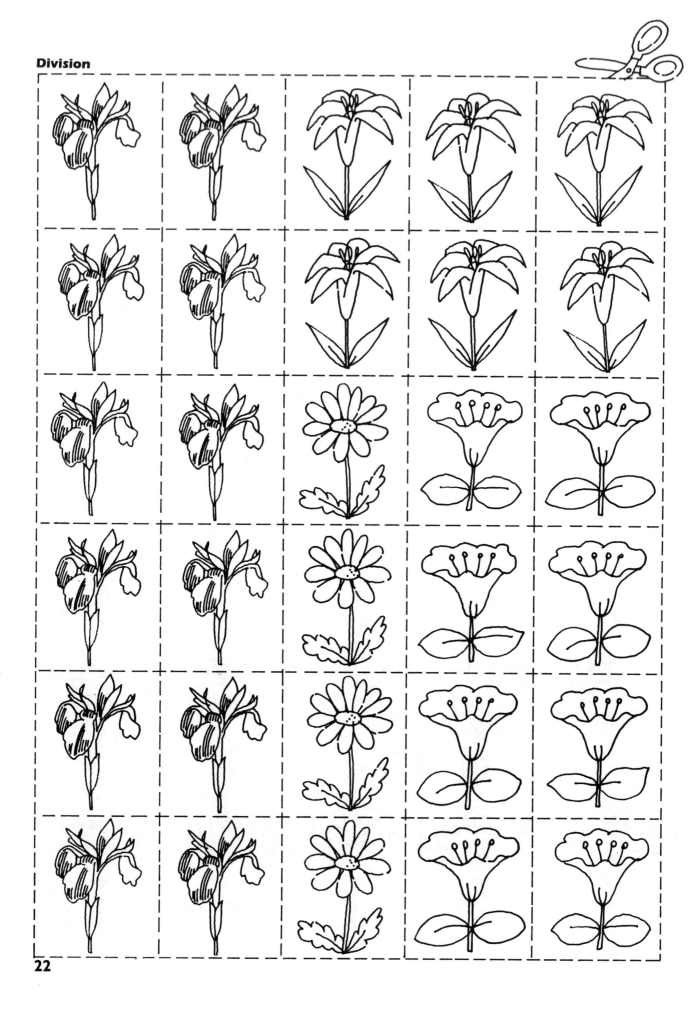

# The Great Divide

**Objective: Understanding division by six through nine**

## What You Need:

**Reproducible** on page 24 for each pair of students

**For sharing:** a few dozen paper baking cups; several dozen counters; yardstick; a dozen (or so) buttons; fact cards for multiplication and division (to nine)

## What You Do:

**1.** Use fact cards, round-robin style, to review multiplication and division facts.

**2.** Again, use the baking cups and counters to model division facts as in the previous lesson. This physical manipulation will help students to understand the concept of dividing a given set of objects into smaller sets.

**3.** Another visual way to model division facts is by using a yardstick for demonstration. If the fact is 16 ÷ 4, place a button at 16 on the yardstick. Aloud, count back four and place a button at that number (12). Count back four again and place another button at that number. Continue until you reach zero. Then count the number of buttons you have placed on the yardstick (4). Give each student a turn to solve other division problems using the yardstick method. Keep the yardstick and buttons in an accessible place for students to use when they need to check their work.

**4.** Repeat the "fact family search" from page 19, using all the multiplication and division fact cards. Point out to students that, if they are struggling with a multiplication or division fact, sometimes thinking about another member of the fact family helps.

**5.** Divide the class into teams of two and distribute the **reproducible** on page 24 to each pair. Read the directions aloud. Then tell students to plan a strategy to complete the pages. Compare papers when everyone is done. Ask students to explain the reasoning behind any differences in their answers.

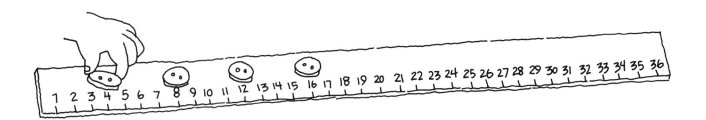

Answers for page 24: 7; 8; 9; 6; 8; 8

Name_____Date_____

# Divide and Escape!

The planet Xelflub is about to explode.  It is your job to decide how many space-ships are needed to get everybody out of there!

| There are: | One spaceship holds: | Spaceships needed: |
|---|---|---|
| 56 Blurfs | 8 Blurfs | |
| 72 Mimmies | 9 Mimmies | |
| 45 Jumpoos | 5 Jumpoos | |
| 42 Heeeps | 7 Heeeps | |
| 48 Quavums | 6 Quavums | |
| 64 Lummers | 8 Lummers | |

Answers on page 23

# Leftovers

**Objective: Understanding remainders with a one-digit divisor**

## What You Need:

**Reproducible** on page 26 for each student

**For sharing:** a few dozen paper baking cups; several dozen counters; thirty to forty index cards with division problems with a one-digit divisor; number cube of any denomination

## What You Do:

**1.** Ask a volunteer to model the division problem 27 ÷ 5 using counters and baking cups. There should be two counters left over. Show how we indicate there are some left over by writing 5 R2 on the chalkboard. Explain that the R represents the leftover amount, or the remainder.

**2.** Place the division problem index cards face-down on the table. Let pairs of students select three or four cards and model the problem with the baking cups and counters. Have them write their answers on a separate sheet of paper. Make the cards, cups, and counters available in class for students to use when they work on division problems.

**3.** Organize students into two teams. One team tosses a number cube and writes a division problem with the resulting number as a remainder. The opposing team checks the division. If the problem is correct, the second team scores a point. Reverse roles. The first team to earn fifteen points is the winner.

**4.** Distribute the **reproducible** on page 26 to the students. Read the directions aloud before students complete the sheets on their own.

Answers for page 26:  4 goose livers; 0 shrimp; 3 steaks; 4 rolls; 2 mushrooms; 5 chickens; 6 pies; 4 brussels sprouts

Name_____ Date_____

# Leftovers Again?

Mr. and Mrs. Hoggington are giving a party. They have invited five other guests.
If each person at the party eats the same amount of each food, how much will the
family pets get to eat later?

| They have this much: | The cat and dog get: |
|---|---|
| 67 goose livers | |
| 49 shrimp | |
| 52 steaks | |
| 39 rolls | |
| 44 mushrooms | |
| 26 chickens | |
| 62 pies | |
| 18 brussels sprouts | |

Answers on page 25

# Remainder Reminder

**Objective: Understanding division with a two-digit divisor**

## What You Need:

**Reproducibles** on pages 28, 29, 30, and 31 (one set per two to four students)

**For each student:** pencil and paper

**For sharing:** place-value blocks; baking cups; red, yellow, blue, and green counters; five number cubes, numbered six and under; posterboard; glue; scissors

## What You Do:

**1.** Write the division problem 114 ÷ 23 on the chalkboard. Ask students to find the answer using any method they like. Make place-value blocks, baking cups and counters, pencils, and paper available. Encourage everyone to compare answers and explain how they got them.

**2.** Divide the class into two teams. One team tosses three number cubes to get a dividend (number to be divided), then tosses two number cubes to get a divisor. The opposing team solves the problem. The score for each problem is the number of the remainder. If the answer is "32 R 15," the score is fifteen points. The first team to reach one hundred points or more wins.

**3.** Put together the Dragon Game from the **reproducibles** on pages 28, 29, 30, and 31. Give the class plenty of time to play the game so they can practice their multiplication and division skills.

**4.** Distribute the **reproducible** on page 32 to the students. Read the directions aloud before students complete the pages individually.

Answers for page 32: 21 rubies; 14 diamonds; 13 gold necklaces; 17 emeralds; 13 gold bars; 4 silver rings. Leftovers: 9 rubies; 21 diamonds; 7 gold necklaces; 19 emeralds; 13 gold bars; 58 silver rings

# Dragon Game

## Instructions and Multiplication Game Cards

Cut out the two halves of the game board and paste them together on a sheet of posterboard. Paste the game cards on posterboard and cut them out. Two to four can play. Give each group a number cube. Give each player four counters in red, yellow, blue, or green. All start in the castle. The object of the game is to get all four of the "knights" to the dragons' caves. Players take turns picking a card and answering the problem. A correct answer earns a toss of the number cube and the right to move one knight that number of steps along the path. An incorrect answer results in no movement.

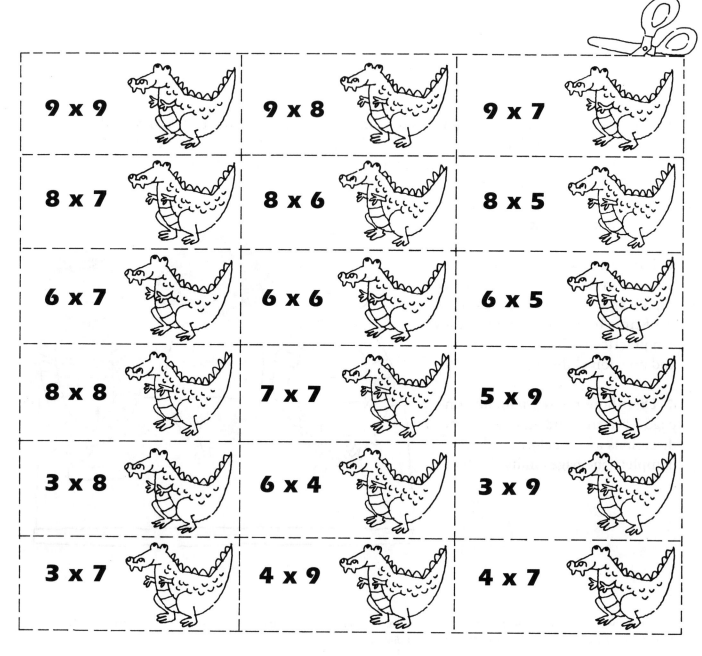

| | | |
|---|---|---|
| 9 x 9 | 9 x 8 | 9 x 7 |
| 8 x 7 | 8 x 6 | 8 x 5 |
| 6 x 7 | 6 x 6 | 6 x 5 |
| 8 x 8 | 7 x 7 | 5 x 9 |
| 3 x 8 | 6 x 4 | 3 x 9 |
| 3 x 7 | 4 x 9 | 4 x 7 |

# Dragon Game

Division Game Cards

| 81 ÷ 9 | 72 ÷ 8 | 72 ÷ 9 |
| --- | --- | --- |
| 64 ÷ 8 | 63 ÷ 7 | 63 ÷ 9 |
| 56 ÷ 7 | 56 ÷ 8 | 54 ÷ 6 |
| 48 ÷ 8 | 49 ÷ 7 | 42 ÷ 6 |
| 35 ÷ 7 | 36 ÷ 4 | 28 ÷ 7 |
| 27 ÷ 3 | 24 ÷ 8 | 24 ÷ 6 |

# Dragon Game

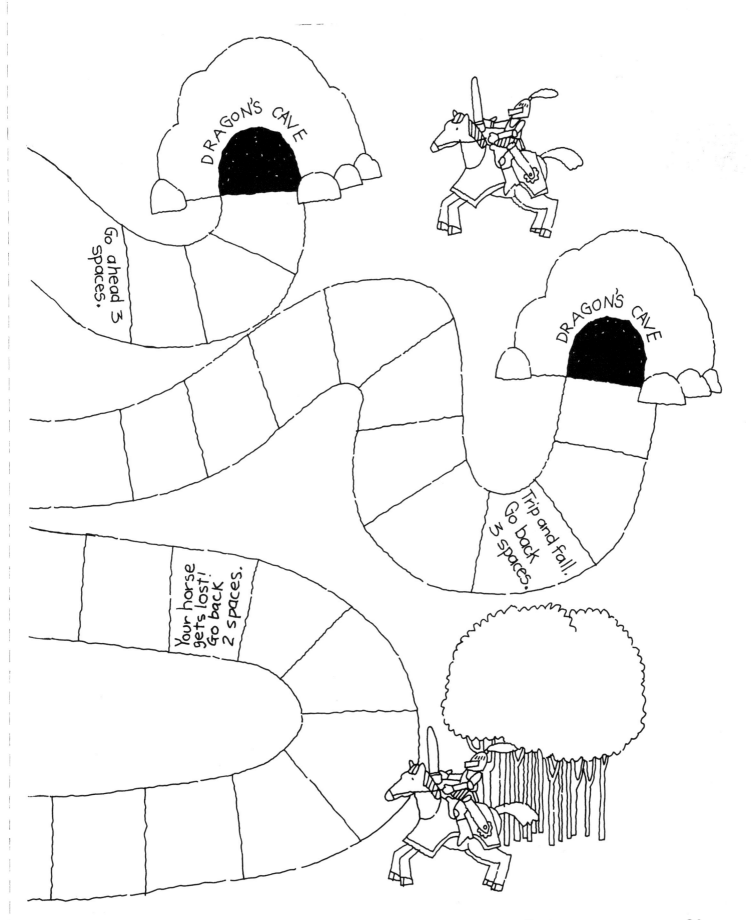

DRAGON'S CAVE

DRAGON'S CAVE

Go ahead 3 spaces.

Trip and fall! Go back 3 spaces.

Your horse gets lost! Go back 2 spaces.

Name_____Date_____

# Joust for Jewels

The King is so happy his team won the jousting tournament that he is giving all his loyal subjects rewards. Find how many precious objects each loyal subject will get and how many jewels will be left over.

| The King is giving: | To: | Each will get: |
|---|---|---|
| 534 rubies | 25 knights | |
| 497 diamonds | 34 ladies-in-waiting | |
| 722 gold necklaces | 55 servants | |
| 648 emeralds | 37 merchants | |
| 819 gold bars | 62 princesses | |
| 294 silver rings | 59 cooks | |

What is left over?

_____ rubies _____ diamonds _____ gold necklaces

_____ emeralds _____ gold bars _____ silver rings

Answers on page 27

# A Piece of the Pie

**Objective: Comparing and ordering fractions**

## What You Need:

**Reproducibles** on pages 34, 35, 36, 37, and 38 for each student

**For sharing:** four index cards drawn with large blue squares; four index cards drawn with small blue squares; four index cards drawn with large red squares; four index cards drawn with small red squares; fraction cards

## What You Do:

**1.** Give each student a set of fraction strips copied from the **reproducibles** on pages 34, 35, 36, and 37. Students can use the fraction strips for many of the fraction activities in this book.

**2.** Lay out five index cards (two with large blue squares and three with large red squares) for everyone to see. Ask the class to name what all the cards have in common. (They are all squares.) Ask "How many are in the set?" (5) "What fraction of the set is blue?" (2/5) "What fraction of the set is red?" (3/5) Select another set of cards and repeat the activity. Change the combinations several times to give the class practice in figuring out fractions.

**3.** After students have practiced naming fractions for the two parts of a set, ask them which fraction is larger. They can count the number of cards in each set. Point out that if the bottom numbers in two fractions are the same, the top numbers will tell them which is larger. Select a pair of fraction cards to show to the students. Ask which fraction is larger. Let the student who answers correctly select the next two fractions to compare.

**4.** Distribute the **reproducible** on page 38 to each student. Read the directions aloud before students work on the sheets individually.

Answers for page 38: 1. $\frac{2}{5}$; 2. $\frac{1}{2}$; 3. $\frac{2}{3}$; 4. $\frac{2}{4}$ ($\frac{1}{2}$); 5. $\frac{3}{5}$; 6. $\frac{1}{3}$; 7. $\frac{3}{4}$; 8. $\frac{5}{8}$; 9. $\frac{1}{4}$

# Fraction Strips

| $\frac{1}{2}$ | $\frac{1}{2}$ | $\frac{1}{4}$ | $\frac{1}{4}$ | $\frac{1}{4}$ | $\frac{1}{4}$ |

| $\frac{1}{8}$ | $\frac{1}{8}$ | $\frac{1}{8}$ | $\frac{1}{8}$ | $\frac{1}{8}$ | $\frac{1}{8}$ | $\frac{1}{8}$ | $\frac{1}{8}$ | $\frac{1}{16}$ $\frac{1}{16}$ $\frac{1}{16}$ $\frac{1}{16}$ $\frac{1}{16}$ $\frac{1}{16}$ $\frac{1}{16}$ $\frac{1}{16}$ $\frac{1}{16}$ $\frac{1}{16}$ $\frac{1}{16}$ $\frac{1}{16}$ $\frac{1}{16}$ $\frac{1}{16}$ $\frac{1}{16}$ $\frac{1}{16}$ |

# Fraction Strips

| $\frac{1}{2}$ |
| :---: |
| $\frac{1}{2}$ |

| $\frac{1}{4}$ |
| :---: |
| $\frac{1}{4}$ |
| $\frac{1}{4}$ |
| $\frac{1}{4}$ |

| $\frac{1}{8}$ |
| :---: |
| $\frac{1}{8}$ |
| $\frac{1}{8}$ |
| $\frac{1}{8}$ |
| $\frac{1}{8}$ |
| $\frac{1}{8}$ |
| $\frac{1}{8}$ |
| $\frac{1}{8}$ |

| $\frac{1}{16}$ |
| :---: |
| $\frac{1}{16}$ |
| $\frac{1}{16}$ |
| $\frac{1}{16}$ |
| $\frac{1}{16}$ |
| $\frac{1}{16}$ |
| $\frac{1}{16}$ |
| $\frac{1}{16}$ |
| $\frac{1}{16}$ |
| $\frac{1}{16}$ |
| $\frac{1}{16}$ |
| $\frac{1}{16}$ |
| $\frac{1}{16}$ |
| $\frac{1}{16}$ |
| $\frac{1}{16}$ |
| $\frac{1}{16}$ |

# Fraction Strips

| $\frac{1}{3}$ | $\frac{1}{6}$ | $\frac{1}{9}$ | $\frac{1}{12}$ |
|---|---|---|---|
| $\frac{1}{3}$ | $\frac{1}{6}$ | $\frac{1}{9}$ | $\frac{1}{12}$ |
| $\frac{1}{3}$ | $\frac{1}{6}$ | $\frac{1}{9}$ | $\frac{1}{12}$ |
| | $\frac{1}{6}$ | $\frac{1}{9}$ | $\frac{1}{12}$ |
| | $\frac{1}{6}$ | $\frac{1}{9}$ | $\frac{1}{12}$ |
| | $\frac{1}{6}$ | $\frac{1}{9}$ | $\frac{1}{12}$ |
| | | $\frac{1}{9}$ | $\frac{1}{12}$ |
| | | $\frac{1}{9}$ | $\frac{1}{12}$ |
| | | $\frac{1}{9}$ | $\frac{1}{12}$ |
| | | | $\frac{1}{12}$ |
| | | | $\frac{1}{12}$ |
| | | | $\frac{1}{12}$ |

# Fraction Strips

Name_____Date_____

# Fraction Critters

These are very rare Fraction Critters. Write the fraction that shows how much of
each Fraction Critter is striped.

**1.**

**2.**

**3.**

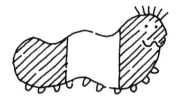

**4.**

**5.**

**6.**

**7.**

**8.**

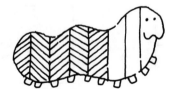

**9.**

Make two of your own Fraction Critters. Let a friend write the fractions.

Answers on page 33

# What's in a Name?

## Objective: Understanding equivalent fractions

## What You Need:

**Reproducible** on page 35 for demonstration

**Reproducible** on page 40 for each student

## What You Do:

**1.** Use the **reproducible** on page 35 for this demonstration. Whisper the following instructions to four students as they pass around the worksheet: tell one student to color 1/2 of the halves strip, another to color 2/4 of the fourths strip, another to color 4/8 of the eighths strip, and the last to color 8/16 of the sixteenths strip. Each student writes the correct fraction for how much is colored. Show the completed sheet to the class. Ask what is the same about the squares (the colored area in each is the same size) and what is different (the fraction describing the colored area). Explain that these are called equivalent fractions because they are different names for the same set.

**2.** Here's an easy way to find an equivalent of a fraction. Write the fraction 3/4 on the board. Explain that if you multiply the numerator and the denominator by the same number, you will have an equivalent fraction. You can multiply 3/4 by 2 to get 6/8, for example. Draw two equal squares on the board. Ask two volunteers to divide one square into four equal parts and the other into eight equal parts. Both should color in the amount shown by the fractions 3/4 and 6/8. The colored areas are the same, so the fractions are equivalent.

**3.** Use the fraction strips to find equivalent fractions. Demonstrate how to align the strips to see if the lines are exactly in the same place.

**4.** Distribute the **reproducible** on page 40 to each student. Read the directions aloud before students complete the sheets on their own. Allow students to use scrap paper to draw models in completing the problems.

Answers for page 40: C, C, B; A, B, A

Name_____Date_____

# Fraction Finish

All the drivers, race cars, tires, and mechanics are mixed up! Put the right drivers, cars, mechanics, and tires together by matching the equivalent fractions. The first example is done for you.

| Car A | Car B | Car C |
|:---:|:---:|:---:|
|  |  |  |

| Driver A | Driver B | Driver C |
|:---:|:---:|:---:|
|  |  |  |

| Mechanic A | Mechanic B | Mechanic C |
|:---:|:---:|:---:|
|  |  |  |

| Tires A | Tires B | Tires C |
|:---:|:---:|:---:|
|  |  |  |

|  | Car | Tires | Mechanic |
|---|:---:|:---:|:---:|
| Driver A | B | A | C |
| Driver B |  |  |  |
| Driver C |  |  |  |

Answers on page 39

# In Other Words

**Objective: Understanding lowest-terms fractions**

## What You Need:

Fraction strips from **reproducibles** on pages 34, 35, 36, 37

**Reproducible** on page 42 for each student

## What You Do:

**1.** Draw three fraction strips on the chalkboard as students use their own fraction strips to follow along. Align the strips so that one shows halves, one shows fourths, and one shows eighths. Shade in 1/2, 2/4, and 4/8 and write those fractions on the side. Ask, "Are these equivalent fractions?" (Yes.) "How can we tell?" (The parts are all the same size.) "Which do you think would be easier to work with?" (1/2, because the numbers are smaller.) Explain that 1/2 is called a lowest-terms fraction.

**2.** Ask students to use their fraction strips to find the lowest-terms fraction for 12/16. Encourage them to find all the possible equivalent fractions and then decide which is the lowest-terms fraction. Repeat this activity several more times, ending with a fraction such as 7/11, which is already a lowest-terms fraction. Point out that in lowest-terms fractions, the numerator and the denominator have no common factors except 1.

**3.** You may find it quite helpful to make up a large set of fraction strips to display on the bulletin board as a convenient reference.

**4.** Distribute the **reproducible** on page 42 to the students. Make sure everyone has a set of fraction strips to help complete the sheet. Read the directions aloud before students complete their sheets individually.

Answers for page 42 (reading down left column first): 5/6; 1/2; 8/11; 3/4; 7/8; 4/5; 2/3; 3/7

Name_____ Date_____

# Simply Wonderful Wibbles

The Wibble sisters, Wanda, Wallie, and Wilma, have finally perfected their formula for jet-broom fuel. Help them write the formula using lowest-terms fractions, so that they can make it more easily.

## The Wibbles' Recipe

10/12 can of bat toes
8/16 jar of toad mud
8/11 can of butterfly spots
9/12 vat of snake oil

14/16 vat of lizard tails
8/10 bag of hens' teeth
6/9 bunch of cat whiskers
3/7 jar of fish eyes

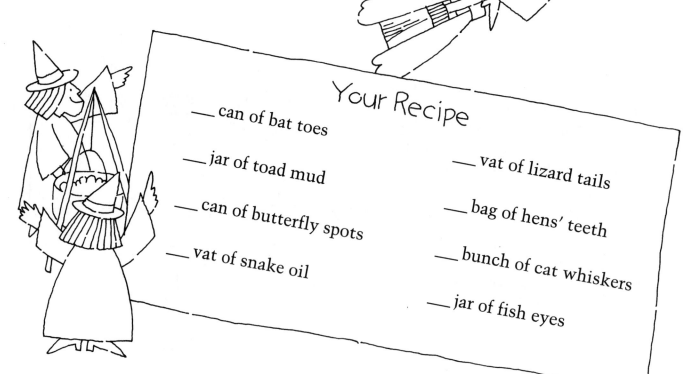

## Your Recipe

___ can of bat toes

___ jar of toad mud

___ can of butterfly spots

___ vat of snake oil

___ vat of lizard tails

___ bag of hens' teeth

___ bunch of cat whiskers

___ jar of fish eyes

Answers on page 41

# The Sum Total

**Objective: Understanding addition of fractions with like denominators**

## What You Need:

Fraction strips from **reproducibles** on pages 34, 35, 36, 37

**Reproducible** on page 44 for each student

**For sharing:** a few dozen buttons

## What You Do:

**1.** Demonstrate addition of fractions by placing eight buttons (or counters or other small objects) on the table. Ask students to tell you how many are in the set (8). Now make a pile of three buttons and a pile of two buttons. Ask students what fraction of the set each pile represents (3/8, 2/8). Push the piles together and ask students to name the fraction of the set this new pile represents (5/8). Point out that the two numerators were added together, but the denominator remained the same. Students should be able to see that the number of buttons in the original set never changed; only the number of buttons in the fraction changed.

**2.** Use fraction strips to model the addition of fractions. Have students use their own fraction strips to follow along with your example. Write the addition problem 3/7 + 2/7 on the chalkboard. Show the sevenths fraction strip. Tell everyone: "First we have 3/7. Find 3/7 on the fraction strip. Then add 2/7 by counting over 2 more sevenths. How many sevenths do we have in all?" (5/7) Repeat the activity several more times. Ask interested children to make up problems for the class.

**3.** Distribute the **reproducible** on page 44 to each student. Read the directions aloud before students complete the sheets individually. Encourage everyone to use the fraction strips to figure out answers.

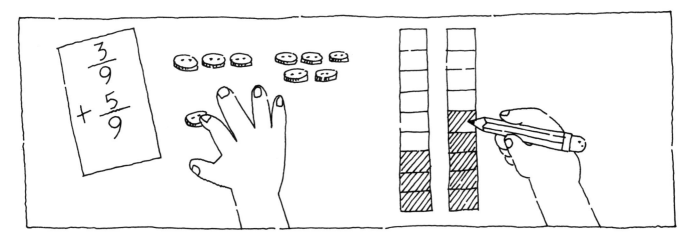

Answers for page 44: 9/10; 11/12; 2/3; 5/8; 2/100 or 1/50

Name_____ Date_____

# All You Can Add

The three Hoggoodle brothers, Bogg, Togg, and Fogg, found a restaurant that serves "All You Can Eat" for just $3.99. Poor restaurant! They will find out the hard way how much the brothers can eat. Find the total amount of food eaten by Bogg, Togg, and Fogg.

|  | Bogg ate: | Togg ate: | Fogg ate: |
|---|---|---|---|
| **lasagna** | 3/10 | none | 6/10 |
| **pies** | 6/12 | 3/12 | 2/12 |
| **spaghetti** | 1/3 | 1/3 | none |
| **bread** | 3/8 | none | 2/8 |
| **peas** | 1/100 | 1/100 | none |

Altogether, the boys ate:

___ of the lasagna

___ of the pies

___ of the spaghetti

___ of the bread

___ of the peas

Answers on page 43

# A Likely Lesson

**Objective: Understanding subtraction of fractions with like denominators**

## What You Need:

**Reproducible** on page 46 for each student

**For sharing:** eight buttons; fraction strips

## What You Do:

**1.** Use the eight buttons to demonstrate the subtraction of fractions. Ask students to name the set (8). Next, form a smaller pile of six buttons from the set and ask the students to identify the fraction this pile represents (6/8). Tell everyone, "Now I am going to subtract a fraction of the buttons. I will subtract 2/8 of the buttons." Move two of the six buttons from the pile and place them at the side. Ask, "What fraction of the set is left?" (4/8) Repeat this activity several more times, using different numbers of buttons.

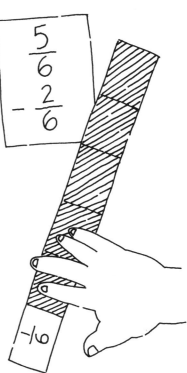

**2.** Again, refer to the fraction strips to help the children model subtraction with fractions. The strips can be used like a number line. Start at the number that represents the numerator of the first fraction and count back the number of the numerator of the second fraction. For example, to find 8/10 - 4/10, start with the tenths fraction strip. Place a marker at the eighth tic mark. Then count back, "One, two, three, four." You will land on the fourth tic mark. (8/10 - 4/10 = 4/10)

**3.** Many students get confused by fractional subtraction because they cannot always *see* the whole set before they are presented with a fraction. For students who erroneously calculate "6/8 - 3/8 = 3/6," emphasize that there is always the same number in the whole set whether we add or subtract. Try modeling with the buttons so students can see that the number in the whole set does not change.

**4.** Distribute the **reproducible** on page 46 to each student. Make sure everyone has sets of fractions strips available. Read the directions aloud before children work on their own to complete the sheets.

Answers for page 46: 1/12; 6/10 (3/5); 8/12 (2/3); 5/9; 6/11; 5/8; 7/12; 36/53

Name_____Date_____

# All Used Up

The Dinglefroozles are having their house painted and cleaned.
How much of each cleaning and painting product has the painter used up?

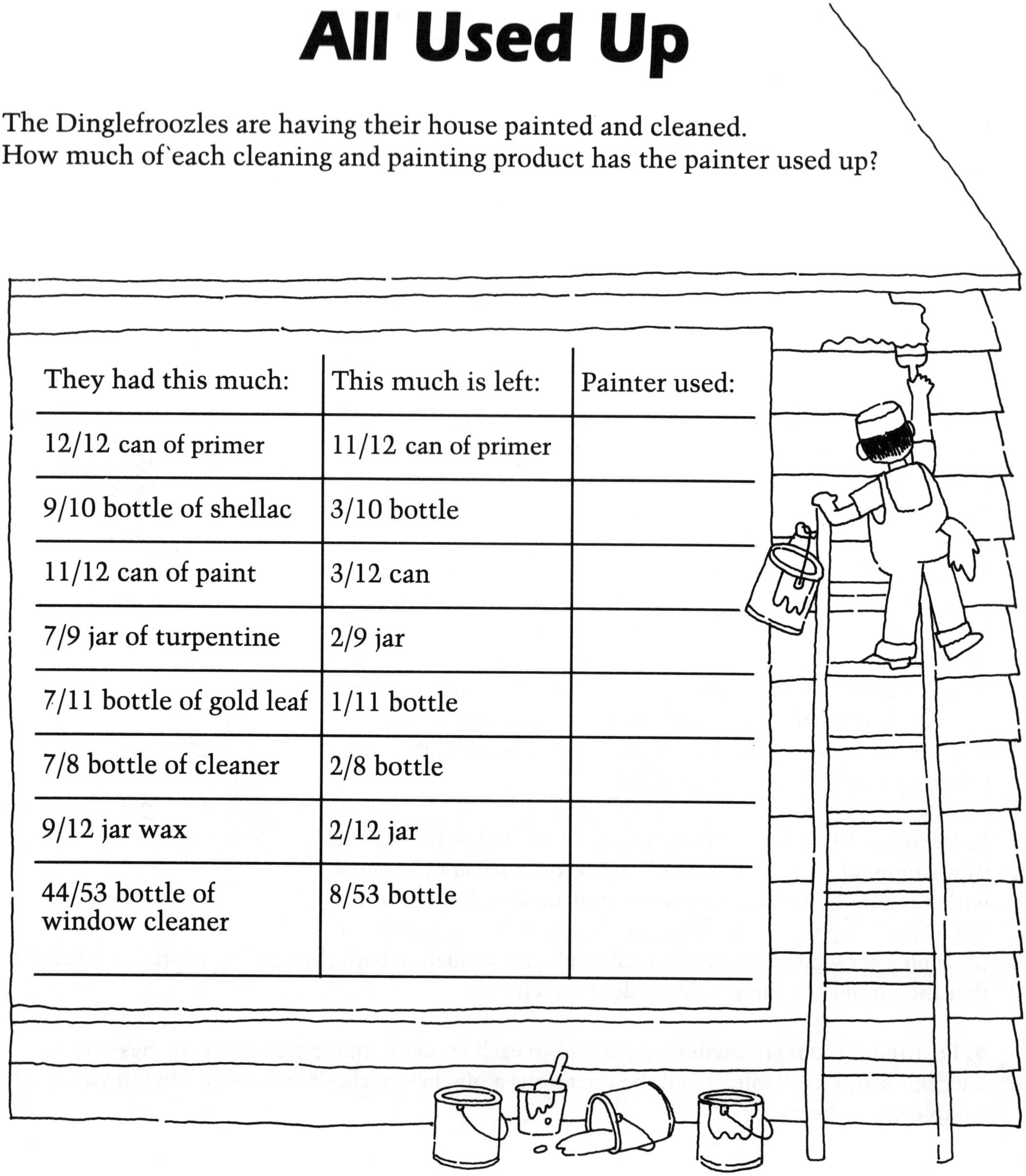

| They had this much: | This much is left: | Painter used: |
| --- | --- | --- |
| 12/12 can of primer | 11/12 can of primer | |
| 9/10 bottle of shellac | 3/10 bottle | |
| 11/12 can of paint | 3/12 can | |
| 7/9 jar of turpentine | 2/9 jar | |
| 7/11 bottle of gold leaf | 1/11 bottle | |
| 7/8 bottle of cleaner | 2/8 bottle | |
| 9/12 jar wax | 2/12 jar | |
| 44/53 bottle of window cleaner | 8/53 bottle | |

Answers on page 45

# What's the Point?

**Objective: Comparing and ordering decimals**

## What You Need:

**Reproducible** on page 48 for each student

**For each student:** pencil and paper

**For sharing:** a one-dollar bill, ten dimes, four quarters, two half-dollars, twenty nickels, one hundred pennies; fraction strip for tenths; one paper bag

## What You Do:

**1.** Tell the class that they already know about decimals if they know about money. Show them a one-dollar bill and write "$1.00" on the chalkboard. Show a penny, nickel, dime, quarter, and half-dollar and write their corresponding values on the board. (*$0.01, $0.05, $0.10, $0.25, and $0.50*) Explain that the period is called a *decimal point* and that it shows that the values to its right are part of one (dollar). Explain that the place-value names to the right of the decimal are tenths and hundredths—opposite of the order to the left of the decimal point.

**2.** Show the tenths fraction strip to the class. Explain that this strip can show decimals, too. Fold the strip to show three parts of the ten on the strip and have students write the decimal equivalent.

**3.** Play a decimal game, with four children per round. Begin by placing a variety of coins in a bag. Each student, in turn, takes a handful of coins and writes the decimal equivalent of their total value. The coins are returned to the bag, and the next student draws. The person with the largest decimal of the four players in three consecutive rounds of play is the winner.

**4.** Distribute the **reproducible** on page 48 to each student. Read the directions aloud before each student completes the sheet individually.

Answers for page 48: 1. 8.33; 2. 8.49; 3. 8.68; 4. 8.78; 5. 8.86; 6. 8.91; FRIZLAPY

Name_____ Date_____

# Out of this World

These aliens tried out for the starring role in a new outer-space movie. The director gave points for how well the aliens could sing, dance, act, and look "out of this world." Write the scores in order from lowest to highest.

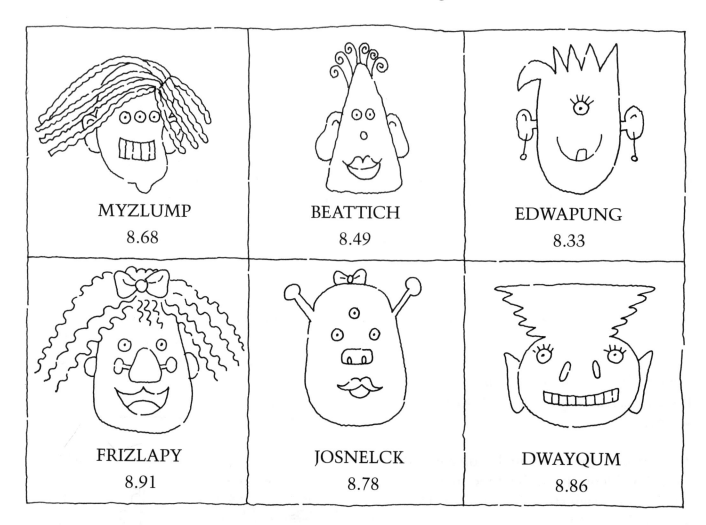

| MYZLUMP | BEATTICH | EDWAPUNG |
| 8.68 | 8.49 | 8.33 |
| FRIZLAPY | JOSNELCK | DWAYQUM |
| 8.91 | 8.78 | 8.86 |

1. _____        2. _____        3. _____

4. _____        5. _____        6. _____

Who will be the new star of "Out of This World?"_____

Answers on page 47

# Get the Point

**Objective:** Adding decimals

## What You Need:

**Reproducible** on page 50 for each student

**For each student:** pencil and sheet of paper

**For sharing:** 25 index cards showing *two* each of random decimal numbers and one card marked "Free"

## What You Do:

**1.** Remind everyone that adding decimals is just like adding money without the dollar sign. The decimal point must still be carried down to the answer. Ask how the addition might be different. (There may be a different number of places to the right of the decimal point, rather than the two used in money amounts.) Explain that the decimal points must always line up. It may help to add zeros to the "shorter" number so all digits align.

**2.** Mix up the numbered index cards and the "Free" card, placing them facedown on a table in rows of five by five. Play a game of "Concentration" with the class. If a student correctly matches two cards, he or she gets to keep them. The "Free" card matches any other card but has no value in determining the winner. The winner is the person whose cards add up to the greatest sum.

**3.** Distribute the **reproducible** on page 50 to each student. Read the directions aloud before students complete the sheets on their own.

Answers for page 50: 1. 70.13; 2. 72.22; 3. 160.01; 4. 87.84; 5. 74.05

Name_____ Date_____

# How Far?

This map shows the distance between planets in light urgs.  Study the map.  Then answer the questions.

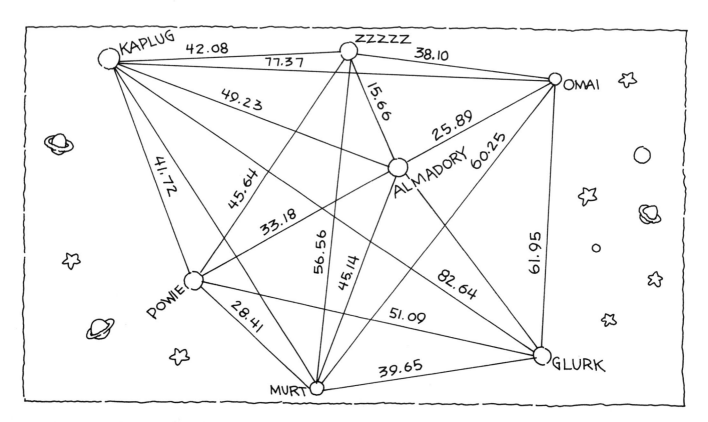

**1.** How far is it from Kaplug to Powie to Murt? _____

**2.** How far is it from Murt to Zzzzz to Almadory? _____

**3.** How far is it from Glurk to Kaplug to Omai? _____

**4.** How far is it from Almadory to Omai to Glurk? _____

**5.** How far is it from Murt to Powie to Zzzzz? _____

Answers on page 49

# Just a Little Less

**Objective: Subtracting decimals**

## What You Need:

**Reproducible** on page 52 for each student

**For each student:** pencil and paper

**For sharing:** three number cubes (one blue, two red); empty boxes marked with prices; play money

## What You Do:

**1.** Ask students to explain how subtracting decimals is like subtracting money. (The decimal points must be aligned.) Then ask how it is different. (There is no dollar sign; there may be a different number of places after the decimal point.) Remind everyone that decimal points must be aligned and carried down when adding or subtracting.

**2.** Organize students into groups of two to four children to play a decimal subtraction game. Each player in turn tosses three number cubes (one blue and two red) twice. The blue cube represents a whole number, and the red cubes represent decimal numbers which can be arranged in any order. The player should subtract the smaller number from the larger number. After each player has had a turn, the one with the difference closest to 1.00 is the winner. You can vary this number to keep the game fresh.

**3.** Set up a class store where students can play "shopkeeper." Put prices on empty boxes (cereal, pasta, cookie, cracker, shoe, and tissue boxes work fine). Arrange them in a corner of the room. Students can take turns playing "shopkeeper" and making change for the others' purchases with the play money. The shoppers are responsible for seeing that they receive the correct change.

**4.** Distribute the **reproducible** on page 52 to each student. Read the directions aloud before students complete the sheets on their own.

Answers for page 52: 1. 4.75; 2. 5.35; 3. 11.81; 4. 5.59; 5. 6.39; 6. 5.61

Name_____ Date_____

# How Much Did They Lose?

Around 64,397 B.C. it became fashionable for dinosaurs to be very thin. All the dinosaurs went on a diet. Find out how much weight each dinosaur lost.

**1. Mr. Bronto**

Used to weigh 54.27 boulders.
Now weighs 49.52 boulders.
He lost _____

**2. Ms. Bronto**

Used to weigh 49.55 boulders.
Now weighs 44.2 boulders.
She lost _____

**3. Mr. T. Rex**

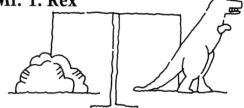

Used to weigh 85.33 boulders.
Now weighs 73.52 boulders.
He lost _____

**4. Ms. T. Rex**

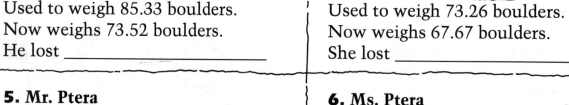

Used to weigh 73.26 boulders.
Now weighs 67.67 boulders.
She lost _____

**5. Mr. Ptera**

Used to weigh 38.35 boulders.
Now weighs 31.96 boulders.
He lost _____

**6. Ms. Ptera**

Used to weigh 34.61 boulders.
Now weighs 29 boulders.
She lost _____

Answers on page 51

# Shape Up!

**Objective:** **Understanding three-dimensional shapes (cube, sphere, triangular pyramid, rectangular pyramid, triangular prism, rectangular prism)**

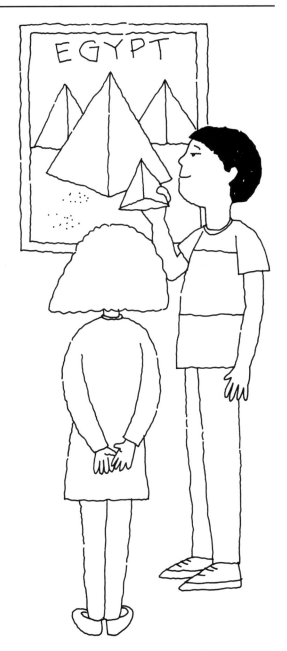

## What You Need:

**Reproducible** on page 54 for each student

**For each student:** pencil and paper

**For demonstration:** picture of an Egyptian pyramid; a variety of solid shape models; pictures of skyscrapers

## What You Do:

**1.** As you show students all the shape models, ask them to name each shape (cube, sphere, triangular pyramid, triangular prism, rectangular pyramid, rectangular prism). Then ask why these are called "three-dimensional" shapes. (They all have height, width, and depth.) Ask one volunteer to come to the front of the room and point out the height, width, and depth of a cube. Repeat, using other students for each shape.

**2.** Display a picture of an Egyptian pyramid. Ask "What do we call the basic shape of this structure? Why?" (It is a rectangular pyramid, because the base is a rectangle, and it has four faces.) Display pictures of skyscrapers and ask the children to name the basic shape or shapes. (Many buildings can be broken down into several diminishing rectangular prisms.)

**3.** Ask students to make up riddles for one another, such as "I am a three-dimensional figure. I have no base. I have no faces. I have no edges or vertices. What am I?" (A sphere)

**4.** Distribute the **reproducible** on page 54 to each student. Read the directions aloud before students complete the sheets individually.

Name_____Date_____

# Shipshape Search

Find objects in your neighborhood that have these basic shapes.

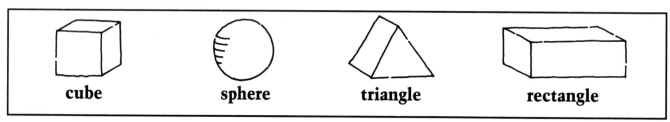

| cube | sphere | triangle | rectangle |

Draw each example you find in the box.

Which shape is the most common?_____

# Scaling Down

**Objective: Understanding scale drawings**

## What You Need:

**Reproducibles** on pages 56 and 57 for each student

**For each student:** pencil; sheet of 1" grid paper; ruler

**For demonstration:** Scale drawings from atlases, encyclopedias, home magazines, and newspaper real-estate sections; large posterboard; thick black marker; tracing paper (same size as posterboard) marked off in 5" squares

## What You Do:

**1.** To help students understand the concept of scale, show them scale drawings of rooms or houses from home magazines, as well as scale drawings of geographic features in an atlas or encyclopedia. Explain that scale drawings are precisely reduced versions of larger pictures. Tell the class you are going to make an oversized drawing and then show how everyone can copy it to scale.

**2.** On a large piece of posterboard, use a thick black marker to draw a large outline of a building, a face, or a tree. Over the drawing, tape a piece of tracing paper on which you have already drawn 5" grids. Trace the picture onto the tracing paper. Point out to the class that every part of the picture underneath is represented inside a grid section on the tracing paper.

**3.** Distribute a sheet of 1" grid paper to each student. Explain that if they copy one square at a time from the tracing paper, students can easily reproduce the picture you drew, on a smaller scale. After the pictures are complete, discuss how to write a scale that explains the reduction. *(5" = 1")* Display everyone's pictures on the bulletin board next to the original.

**4.** Distribute the **reproducibles** on pages 56 and 57 to each student. Read the directions aloud before students finish the sheets individually.

Answers for page 56: 1. 7; 2. 6; 3. 4; 4. 5; 5. 9

Answer for page 57: Treasure is approximately 1" west of palm tree

Name_____ Date_____

# How Far Is It, Really?

Look at the map and read the scale.  Use a ruler to help answer the questions.

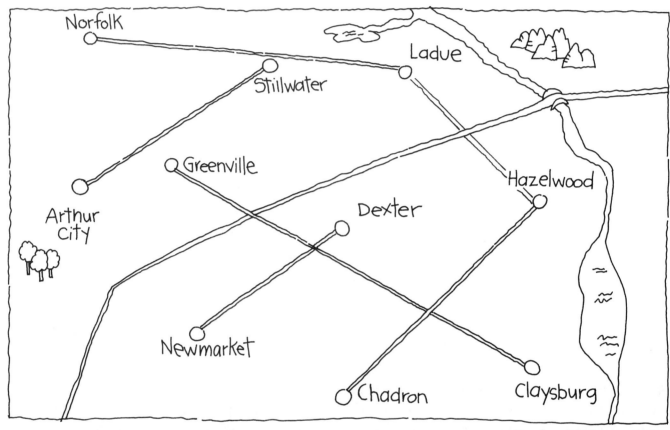

Scale: 1/2" = 1 mile

**1.** How far is it from Norfolk to Ladue? _____

**2.** How far is it from Hazelwood to Chadron? _____

**3.** How far is it from Dexter to Newmarket? _____

**4.** How far is it from Arthur City to Stillwater? _____

**5.** How far is it from Greenville to Claysburg? _____

Answers on page 55

Name_____Date _____

# Find the Treasure

Captain Short Fred Gold left these directions to his buried treasure.  Find the treasure.  Put an X on the map to mark the spot.

> Start at the east side of the palm tree.  Go 6 paces north.  Then go 8 paces west.  Then go north until you find a large rock.  Go 5 paces east.  Then go 10 paces south.  Dig down 6 feet.

Scale: 1/2" = 1 pace

Answer on page 55

# Arranging Shapes

**Objective: Understanding tangrams**

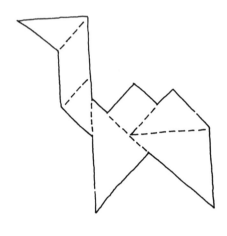

## What You Need:

**Reproducibles** on pages 59 and 60 for each student

**For each student:** one 8 1/2" x 11" piece of poster-board; one letter-size envelope; one sheet of paper

**For sharing:** scissors; glue; pencils; crayons

## What You Do:

**1.** Distribute the **reproducible** on page 59 to each student, along with a piece of posterboard and an envelope. Have students paste the tangram patterns on the posterboard and then cut out all the pieces. Have them write their names on the back of each piece as well as on an envelope. The pieces can be colored and kept in the envelope for future use.

**2.** Ask students whether they can remember how all the pieces fit together to form the large square on the original sheet. Ask a volunteer to put together his or her pieces into the original square.

**3.** Hand out the **reproducible** on page 60 to each student. Read the directions aloud before students complete the activity individually or as partners.

**4.** After students have completed the tangram sheets, encourage everyone to experiment with their tangrams. If they make an interesting shape, they can draw the outline on a sheet of paper and challenge others in the class to make that shape, too.

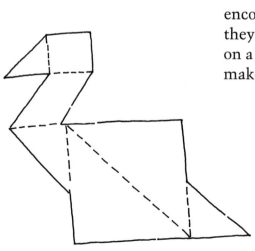

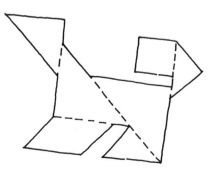

# Make-A-Tangram Pattern

Paste this sheet onto a piece of posterboard. Cut out and save these pieces for tangram activities.

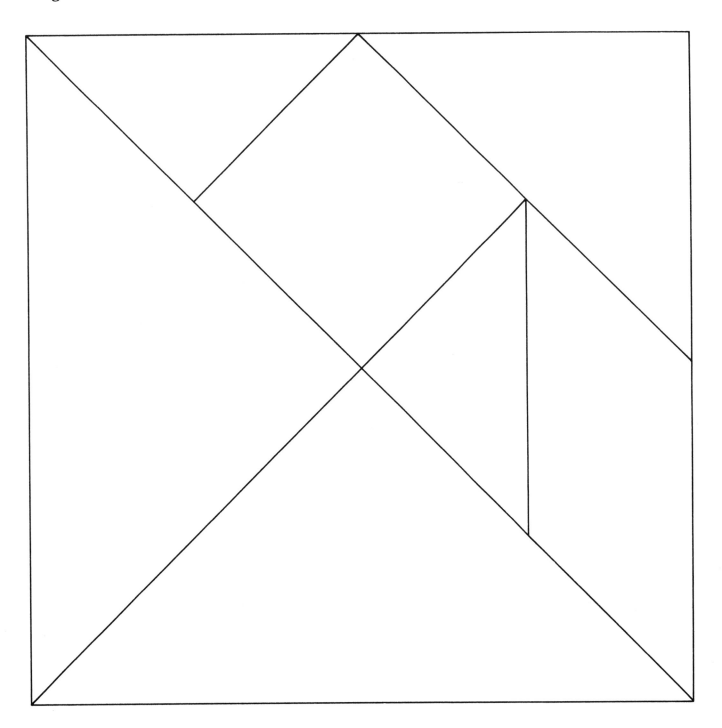

# Tangram Art

Use your tangram pieces to copy these models.

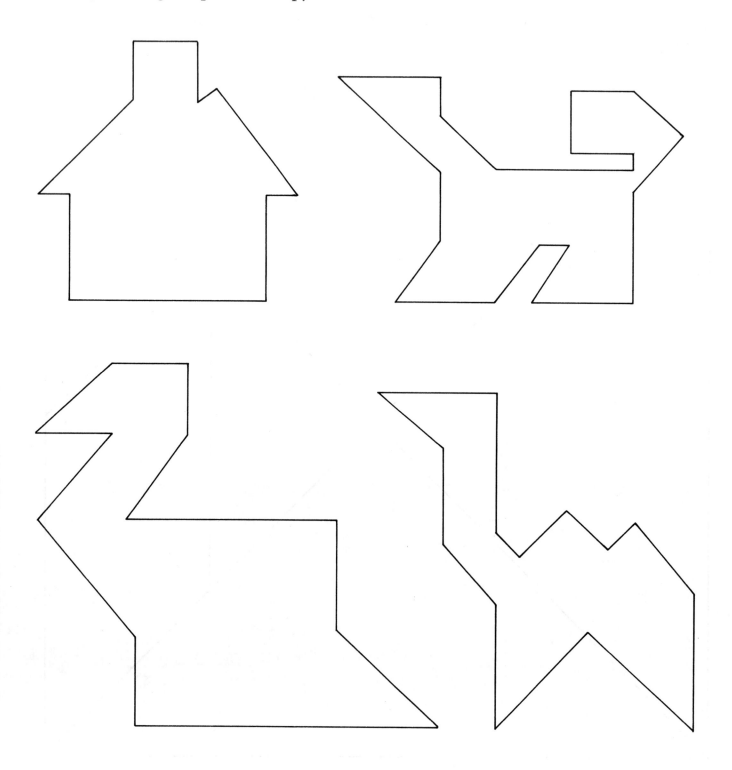

# All the Way Around

**Objective: Understanding perimeter**

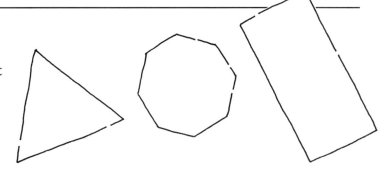

## What You Need:

**Reproducible** on page 62 for each student

**For each student:** pencil and paper

**For sharing:** rulers and/or yardsticks

## What You Do:

**1.** Ask four small groups of students to measure the perimeter of the classroom. Distribute rulers and/or yardsticks and assign each group one wall to measure. (If all groups measure clockwise around the room, traffic jams will be minimal.) The groups should record their measurements on the board. Have a volunteer add all the measurements. Ask if there is an easier way to find the distance around the room, or the *perimeter*. If no one knows how, explain that it's possible to measure one length of the room and one width of the room, add those together and multiply by two. Remind the class that this formula for finding the perimeter is true only for parallelograms: four-sided figures whose opposite sides are parallel and equal, such as a square or a rectangle.

**2.** Organize students into small groups to measure the perimeter of other parallelograms in the classroom: doors, windows, desktops, books, tables, chalkboards, bulletin boards, etc. Remind the groups to use the formula for measuring parallelograms. Each group can present their findings to the class and explain their methods.

**3.** Draw an equilateral triangle, an irregular triangle, a parallelogram, a regular hexagon, and a regular octagon. Discuss how many sides of each figure are the same length. Ask the children to determine a formula that might make finding the perimeter of each figure a little easier.

$a$ x 3 = perimeter

$2a + 2b$ = perimeter

$a$ x 6 = perimeter

$a$ x 8 = perimeter

**4.** Distribute the **reproducible** on page 62 to each student. Read the directions aloud before students complete the sheets individually.

Answers for page 62: 1. 10"; 2. 10"; 3. 15"; 4. 13"

Name_____ Date_____

# Don't Fence Me In

Find the perimeter of each field on the farm.  Use your ruler to measure to the nearest 1/2".

Answers on page 61

# Grid Look

**Objective: Understanding area**

## What You Need:

**Reproducible** on page 64 for each student

**For each student:** pencil; sheet of grid paper; colored paper

**For sharing:** scissors; calculators

## What You Do:

**1.** Distribute a sheet of grid paper to each student. Ask everyone to draw three rectangles of differing sizes and cut them out. Ask "How many grid squares are in each rectangle?" Students can count the squares, or use any method they like, to find the answers. After they have found the number of squares, remind them that this is called the *area* of the rectangle. Introduce the formula $a \times b$ = area, where $a$ represents the length of the rectangle and $b$ represents the width. Ask them to find the areas of their rectangles again, this time using the formula. Have them write the formula on each rectangle. They can paste the rectangles on a piece of colored paper and post them on the bulletin board.

**2.** Give students time to examine all the rectangles. Are any of the rectangles similar? Do any of the rectangles have the same area? Are these rectangles all the same shape with the exact same measurements?

**3.** Distribute the **reproducible** on page 64 to each student. Read the directions aloud before students complete the sheet individually. You may want to allow the use of calculators, depending on the learning level of your class.

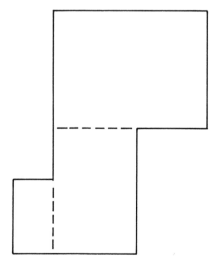

**4.** Draw the figure to the right (without the dotted lines) on the chalkboard.

Ask students how they can find the area of this figure. If they have a difficult time, you may add the dotted lines to give them a clue. By dividing the figure into three rectangles, they can easily find the area of each rectangle and add them together. Ask groups of students to work together to find the area. Allow the use of calculators.

Name_____ Date_____

# Boy, That Stinks!

The 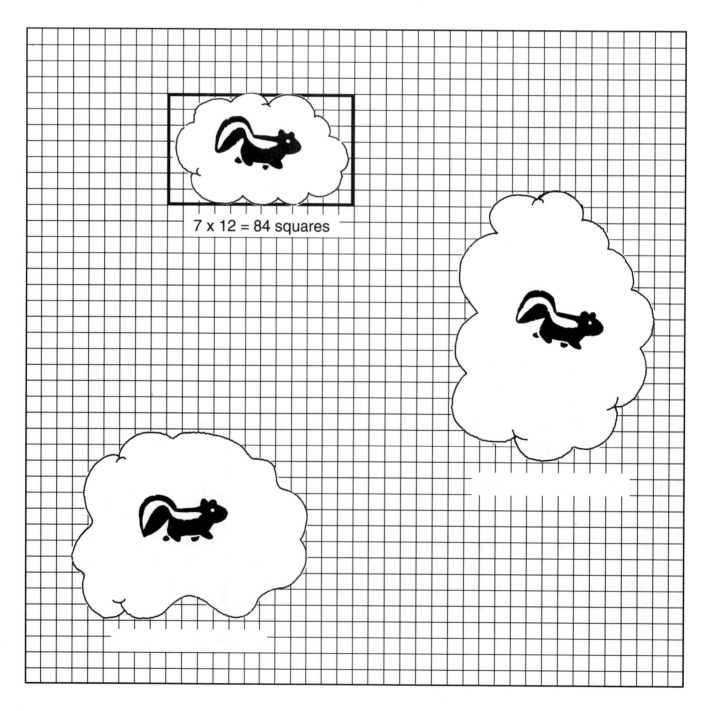shows how far each skunk sprays.  Draw a rectangular fence around each skunk and find its area.  One example is done for you.

7 x 12 = 84 squares

# Speaking Volumes

**Objective: Understanding volume**

## What You Need:

**Reproducible** on page 66 for pairs of students

**For each student:** pencil and paper

**For sharing:** six to eight different rectangular boxes such as shoe, milk, cake, cookie, cracker, pasta, or cereal boxes; rulers; calculators

## What You Do:

**1.** Set aside three of the boxes before showing the class the rest. Remind everyone that the term *volume* tells how much a container holds. The volume of a container is always the same, whether it is filled with air, water, popcorn, or rocks. Explain that the formula for finding the volume of a rectangular prism is: "Length times width times height equals volume." Ask groups of students to measure the boxes and find the volumes in cubic inches. Pass the boxes around so that each group has a chance to work with each box. Allow the use of calculators. Afterwards, have the groups compare answers. If there is a discrepancy, the box can be remeasured. Label all the boxes with their volumes.

**2.** Show students the three other rectangular boxes you had set aside and labeled A, B, and C. Ask each student to compare the boxes with the others and estimate the volume of the new boxes. Each person can record an estimate. Then the class can measure the boxes and calculate the volume. Were any estimates close?

**3.** Distribute the **reproducible** on page 66 to pairs of children in the class. Read the directions at the top of the page together then let partners complete the pages with the help of a calculator.

Answers for page 66: 1. 2,340; 2. 5,940; 3. 16,120; 4. 38,500

Name_____Date_____

# Lots of Hot Air

On the planet Xerbeeg, all the balloons are rectangular prisms. Find the volume of each balloon. How many cubic erks in each? You may use a calculator to figure answers.

**1.** 12 erks long
13 erks wide
15 erks high
volume:

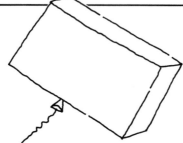

**2.** 22 erks long
18 erks wide
15 erks high
volume:

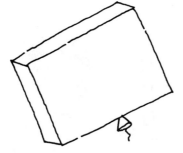

**3.** 31 erks long
26 erks wide
20 erks high
volume:

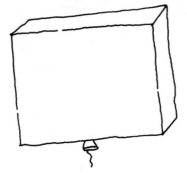

**4.** 35 erks long
25 erks wide
44 erks high
volume:

Answers on page 65

# How Long Did It Take?

**Objective: Understanding elapsed time**

## What You Need:

**Reproducible** on page 68 for each student

**For each student:** pencil and paper

**For demonstration and sharing:** calculators; alarm clock; posterboard

| Subject: | MON. | | TUES. | | WED. | | THUR. | | FRI. |
|---|---|---|---|---|---|---|---|---|---|
| | START | END | START | END | START | END | START | END | |
| Reading | 8:30 | 9:15 | | | | | | | |
| ART | 9:20 | 10:10 | | | | | | | |
| MATH | | | | | | | | | |
| Science | | | | | | | | | |
| Lunch | | | | | | | | | |
| Gym | | | | | | | | | |

## What You Do:

**1.** Pause during a math session and ask, "How long have we been studying math today?" Chances are, most students will not be able to give an exact answer. Ask what they would need to know in order to be able to answer the question (the time they started and the time it is now). Tell them what time they started, and then have them look at the clock for the present time. Allow them to calculate the answer. Later, pause again and ask the same question.

**2.** Secretly, set up an alarm clock in the classroom. As you begin your daily routine, casually say, "It's nine o'clock. It's time to begin our class." When the alarm goes off, ask the children to tell you how long class has been in session.

**3.** Make a poster of class subjects and activities—the time started, the time ended, and the elapsed time. Keep track of times for one week by assigning each student one event on one day. Give that student responsibility for noting the starting and ending times and for calculating the elapsed time. At the end of the week, find how much time was spent on each subject or activity by adding all the elapsed times.

**4.** Distribute the **reproducible** on page 68 to each student. Read the directions at the top of the page aloud before students complete the pages individually.

Answers for page 68: 1. 3 hours/41 minutes;  2. 4 hours/50 minutes;  3. 4 hours/19 minutes;  4. 4 hours/38 minutes;
5. 3 hours/37 minutes;  6. 4 hours/16 minutes;  Harley won the race.

Name_____ Date_____

# The Great Snail Race

In the Great Snail Race, each snail starts at a different time. Find how long it will take each snail to finish the race.

| Snail | Start | Finish | Time |
|---|---|---|---|
|  **1.** Slowpoke | 12:36 | 4:17 | |
|  **2.** Smasher | 12:38 | 5:28 | |
|  **3.** Trotter | 12:40 | 4:59 | |
|  **4.** Zipper | 12:42 | 5:20 | |
|  **5.** Harley | 12:44 | 4:21 | |
|  **6.** Ferarry | 12:46 | 5:02 | |

Which snail won the race? _____

Answers on page 67

# If This Is Math, It Must Be Monday

**Objective: Understanding calendar time**

## What You Need:

**Reproducible** on page 70 for each student

**For each student:** pencil and paper

**For sharing:** dictionary and/or encyclopedia

## What You Do:

**1.** Ask the class to answer this question: "You have been called the class of (correct year). What does that mean?" (The year designated is their graduation year.) Ask the class to figure out how many years away that year is. "How many more years for high school graduation? College?"

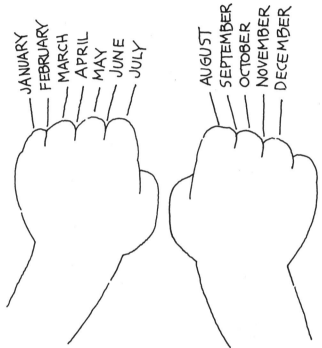

**2.** Show the children an easy way to remember which months have thirty-one days. Make two fists and hold them thumb-side together. If each knuckle and each valley represent one month, all the knuckle months will have thirty-one days. So, January, March, May, July, August, October, and December have thirty-one days.

**3.** Most schools or public buildings have a plaque commemorating their construction. Ask the children to find the date your school was built and to calculate how old the building is. If your school has no plaque, suggest another prominent and accessible building in the area.

**4.** The children might enjoy learning about other uncommon words that we use to denote time spans and the origins of the names of the days and months. Have volunteers look up and report on *fortnight, decade, century, annual, score,* and the days of the week and the months of the year. Add other words as you see fit.

**5.** Distribute the **reproducible** on page 70 to each student. Read the directions aloud before students complete the sheets on their own.

Answers for page 70: July 9, 2847; October 22, 2847; June 28, 2859; March 13, 2860; 3 months, 5 days; 7 months, 13 days; July 3, 2851

Name_____ Date _____

# Future Friends

It is January 1, 2847.  Grump and Grouch are talking about their lives.

**Grump**                              **Grouch**

Grump says, "It is 6 months and 8 days until my birthday."

   When is Grump's birthday?_____

Grouch says, "It is 9 months and 21 days until my birthday."

   When is Grouch's birthday?_____

Grump says, "I can retire in 12 years, 5 months, and 27 days."

   When will Grump retire?_____

Grouch says, "I can retire in 13 years, 2 months, and 12 days."

   When will Grouch retire?_____

Grump says, "This year I get April 6 off from work."

   How long will Grump have to wait for a day off?_____

Grouch says, "This year I get August 14 off from work."

   How long will Grouch have to wait for a day off?_____

Grump says, "I am going to Tahiti in 4 years, 6 months, and 2 days."

   When is Grump going to Tahiti?_____

Grouch says, "Harummmmmph!"

Answers on page 69

# On Time

**Objective: Understanding time schedules**

## What You Need:

**Reproducible** on page 72 for each student

**For each student:** pencil; three sheets of paper; copy of a *TV Guide* page

**For sharing:** copies of other kinds of schedules such as bus, train, or plane schedules, or even your own school schedule

## What You Do:

**1.** Ask the class how they know when their favorite televisions shows are on. They will probably come up with several answers, such as the *TV Guide*, advertisements in the papers, word of mouth, or even, "Because it's on at the same time on the same day every week."

**2.** Distribute a copy of a *TV Guide* prime-time schedule, which looks like a table. Also find a more complex schedule, such as a bus or airline schedule (available from bus companies, airlines, or travel agents) to pass around. Allow the class ample time to examine the schedules, and then review how to use each one. Ask which is easier to read. *(Probably the TV Guide.)* Make up questions for the children to answer, such as, "I want to watch television at 8:30 tonight. What could I watch? When is (specific program) going to be on TV?" Or "I want to go from (place) to (place). What time(s) could I leave? What time(s) could I get there?" After everyone is comfortable reading the schedules, have them make up their own questions for each other. Students may also enjoy looking at your own daily or school-year schedules to see how you plan your time.

**3.** Give each student three sheets of paper and ask them to fold each in half to make a booklet. On the front, have them write their names. Inside, have them write the names of the next few days at the top of each page. They can write down events in their own lives and times that they plan to do things, just as many adults do. At the very least, they can enter "going to school" and "coming home from school" on weekdays. Later, they can write in if the event went as planned, was canceled for rain, was missed, or whatever the results were.

**4.** Distribute the **reproducible** on page 72. Read the directions aloud before students complete the sheet individually.

Answers for page 72: 1. Boot Hill Post Office; 2. Crossroads; 3. 9:25; 4. Railroad Station

Name_____Date_____

# The Naughty Nasty Gang

The Naughty Nasty Gang plans to hold up the Pony Express.
Read the schedule. Then answer the questions below.

| Pony Express Schedule | |
| --- | --- |
| **Time** | **Place** |
| 8:15 | Crossroads |
| 9:25 | Canyon |
| 10:33 | Bottom of Hill |
| 11:10 | Top of Hill |
| 12:05 | Railroad Station |
| 2:15 | Boot Hill Post Office |

**1.** If the Gang feels like robbing about 2:00, where should they wait?

_____

**2.** If the Gang feels like robbing early in the morning, where should they wait?

_____

**3.** If the Gang feels like a trip to the Canyon, what time should they be there?

_____

**4.** If the Gang feels like robbing about noon, where should they wait?

_____

Answers on page 71

# Good Morning

**Objective: Understanding A.M. and P.M.**

## What You Need:
**Reproducible** on page 74 for each student
**For each student:** pencil and paper

## What You Do:
**1.** Explain to the class that the clock goes around twice a day. A.M. is used to indicate the time from midnight to before noon, and P.M. indicates time from noon up to midnight. Call out all types of activities, such as watching cartoons, going to bed, watching a ball game, or going to school. Have the class guess whether each would be an A.M. or P.M. event. Give students a chance to name activities for the whole class to guess.

**2.** Give a sheet of paper to each student. Have everyone fold the sheet in half vertically and write the A.M. hours down the left side and the P.M. hours down the center fold. They should then make a schedule for one weekday. What might they be doing at each hour? Have them compare schedules. Are they all doing the same thing at 2 A.M.? What about 4 P.M.?

**3.** Distribute the **reproducible** on page 74 to each student. Read the directions aloud before students complete the sheets individually.

Answers for page 74:  1. Crunch, Muncher;  2. Chewer, Gobble, Mavis;  3. Crunch, Jaws, Grabber;  4. Chewer, Gobble, Mavis;
5. Crunch, Muncher, Grabber

Name_____Date_____

# Crocodile Watch

This is the schedule for the crocodiles who guard the castle moat.  In the questions below, tell who is on duty at each time.  More than one crocodile may be on duty at one time.

| Name | On Duty |
|------|---------|
| **Crunch** | 8:00 A.M.  -  5:00 P.M. |
| **Muncher** | 12:00 P.M.  -  9:00 P.M. |
| **Chewer** | 6:00 P.M.  -  3:00 A.M. |
| **Gobble** | 8:30 P.M.  -  4:30 A.M. |
| **Jaws** | 2:00 A.M.  -  11:00 A.M. |
| **Grabber** | 6:00 A.M.  -  1:00 P.M. |
| **Mavis** | 10:00 P.M.  -  2:00 A.M. |

**1.** Who is on duty at 3:45 P.M.? _____

**2.** Who is on duty at 11:15 P.M.? _____

**3.** Who is on duty at 8:30 A.M.? _____

**4.** Who is on duty at 1:30 A.M.? _____

**5.** Who is on duty at 12:00 noon? _____

Answers on page 73

# Money, Money

**Objective: Counting and comparing sums of money**

## What You Need:

**Reproducible** on page 76 for each student

**For each student:** pencil and small slip of paper

**For sharing:** play money (coins and bills) or enough real
pennies, dimes, nickels, and quarters to fill four baby-food jars;
a small bag for each group of four students in class;
four baby-food jars; small objects with price tags

## What You Do:

**1.** Prepare a bag of play coins—$8-$10 worth per bag—for groups of four students each, to play
Grab Bag. Without looking, each student grabs a handful of coins from the bag and counts it.
The student who has the amount closest to exactly $1.00 wins that round. In subsequent
rounds, vary the amount needed to win ($1.15, 85¢). For another variation, give one point to
the student with the greatest amount of money, one point to the student with the least
amount of money, and two points to the student whose amount is the closest to the target
amount. The first to get twenty points wins the game.

**2.** Display baby-food jars of equal size, filled with different denominations of play or real
money. One should contain pennies, one nickels, one dimes, and one quarters. The jars
should not be filled up, nor should they be filled to the same level. Ask each student to write
on a slip of paper an estimate of how much money is contained in each jar. After all the slips
are turned in, small groups of students can count the coins in each jar and record the results.
Then compare the estimates to see who came the closest for each jar.

**3.** Display small items with price tags attached. Allow small groups of students to select four
items. The groups can count out the coins that would be needed for each item and place
them next to the item. Then ask the groups to rotate turns around the room. As they check
to see that the previous groups' answers are correct, they put the coins back in the bag. Ask
that they rotate around the room one more time to repeat the activity with a different set of
items.

**4.** Distribute the **reproducible** on page 76 to the students. Read the directions aloud before
students work individually to complete the sheet.

Answers for page 76: 1. 45¢; 29¢, 52¢; 2. $1.04, 99¢; 3. $1.40, $1.39, $1.29

Name_____ Date_____

# Bone Shopping

Count the money in each box.  Circle the dinosaur bones you could buy for each amount.

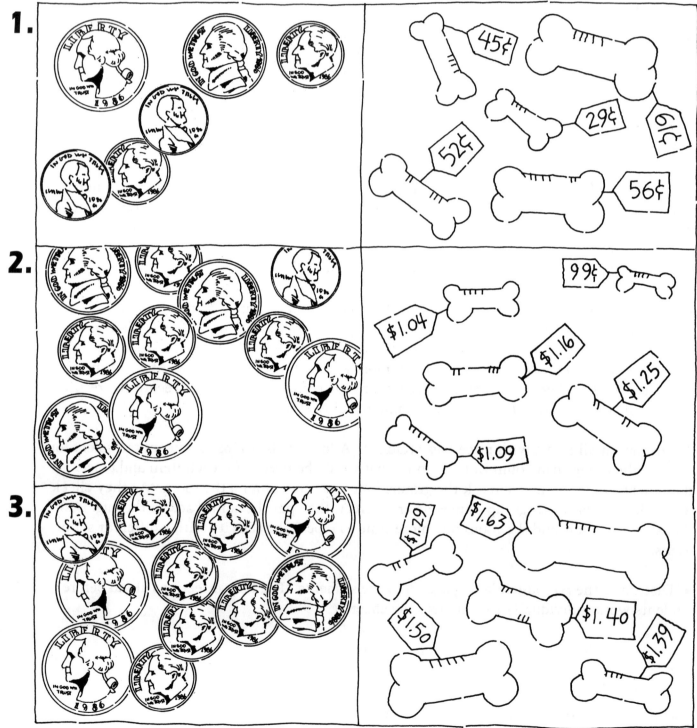

# A Little More, a Little Less

**Objective: Adding and subtracting amounts of money**

## What You Need:

**Reproducible** on page 78 for each student

**For each student:** pencil and paper

**For each group of four students:** paper; a small bag filled with play money, as in activity on page 75

**For sharing:** calculators; two or three old catalogues; scissors; glue

## What You Do:

**1.** Organize groups of four students to play another variation of Grab Bag. As before, each student grabs a handful of coins from the bag, without looking, and counts it. The student with the greatest amount of money gets to keep the amount over that of the next greatest amount. For example, if the amounts are $1.47, $1.63, $1.72, and $1.98, the student who grabbed the $1.98 would keep $1.98 - $1.72 = 26¢. After students win $1.00, they drop out of the game while the others continue to play.

**2.** Add bills to the bag of coins. Again, in groups of four, students draw handfuls of money and count the amount. Then the groups must determine (a) the two amounts with the greatest total value, (b) the two amounts with the least total value, and (c) how to make two combinations of two amounts that come the closest in total value. Each group keeps track of the original amounts and the combinations on a piece of paper. The groups can report on their findings to the rest of the class and explain their methods of solution.

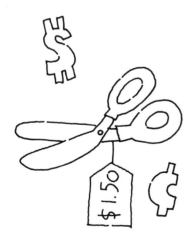

**3.** Ask the students to look through old catalogues and find three items they would like to have. They can cut out the pictures and prices, paste them on a sheets of paper, and find the total cost of the items.

**4.** Distribute the **reproducible** on page 78. Read the directions aloud before students complete the sheets on their own. You may want to allow the use of calculators, depending on the level of your class.

Answers for page 78: 1. $41.85; 2. $28.15; 3. $45.11; 4. $44.89; 5. $52.95; 6. $43.05

Name_____ Date_____

# How Much Change?

The Hazelfloff sisters are Halloween witches. Every October they go shopping. Find out what each sister spent and how much change she got back.

Helga    Hilda    Hulda

**1.** Helga bought a magic potion, a witch spell, a love powder, and a curse.

How much did they cost? _____

**2.** She paid with $70.

How much change did she get? _____

**3.** Hilda bought a curse, a hex, a love powder, a lipstick, and a magic spell.

How much did they cost? _____

**4.** She paid with $90.

How much change did she get? _____

**5.** Hulda bought a mirror, a magic potion, a brew recipe, a broom, and a hex.

How much did they cost? _____

**6.** She paid with $96.

How much change did she get? _____

Answers on page 77

# Above Average

**Objective: Understanding multiplication and division of money**

## What You Need:

**Reproducible** on page 80 for each student

**For each group of four students:** a small bag filled with play money as on page 75

**For sharing:** calculators; two strips or sheets of postage stamps in two different denominations; packaged food such as bread, sliced cheese, a dozen eggs, or a box of doughnuts, with price stickers

## What You Do:

**1.** Show the class a sheet of postage stamps. Explain that each stamp costs the same (for instance, 29¢), and that there are ___ stamps in the sheet. Ask how you might find the cost of the sheet. (Multiply the cost of one stamp by the total number of stamps.) Display the back of another sheet of stamps (or the front, if there is no price shown) and tell the children that this sheet cost ____, and that there are ___ stamps in this sheet. Ask how you might find the cost of one stamp. (Divide the total price by the number of stamps.) Ask for volunteers to work out answers on a calculator.

**2.** Show the class how to average several amounts by adding them together and dividing the total by the number of amounts. Then, organize the class into groups of four and give each group a bag of play money. Each student takes out a small handful of money from the bag and counts it. The group members add their amounts together and divide by four to find the average amount they took out. Allow the children to use calculators. Write the answers on the chalkboard.

**3.** Show the class a package of food with a price sticker and count the number of food items inside the package. Ask students to figure out the price of an individual item (one slice of bread, one roll, one doughnut, one slice of cheese).

**4.** Distribute the **reproducible** on page 80. Read the directions aloud before students complete the sheets individually. Have calculators available for students who need them.

Answers for page 80: 1. $214.80; 2. $258.34; 3. $6.22; 4. $292.79; 5. $165.87

Name_____ Date_____

# On Your Toes!

Mr. Floodle works as a toe inspector.  Find how much he earns.

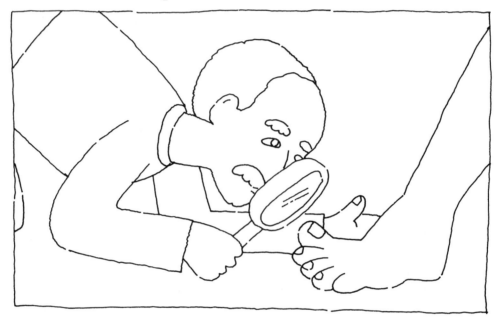

**1.** Mr. Floodle earns $5.37 per hour.  He worked 40 hours this week.  How much did he

earn?_____

**2.** Last week, he worked 43 hours and got a bonus of $27.43.  How much did he

earn?_____

**3.** Next week Mr. Floodle is getting a raise.  He expects to earn $248.80 for working 40

hours. What does he earn per hour?_____

**4.** Mr. Floodle gets a bonus of 83¢ for each ugly toe he finds.  What will he make next

week if he works 40 hours and finds 53 ugly toes? _____

**5.** The following week, Mr. Floodle will be on vacation.  He will get two-thirds of his reg-

ular salary.  How much will he get?_____

Answers on page 79

# It's on the Table

**Objective:** Reading and making tables

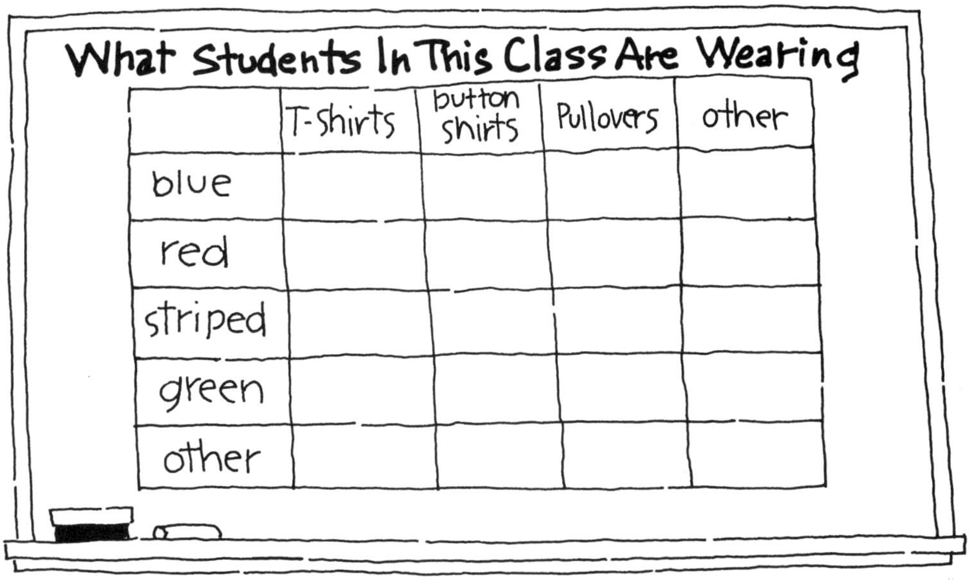

## What Students In This Class Are Wearing

| | T-shirts | button shirts | Pullovers | other |
|---|---|---|---|---|
| blue | | | | |
| red | | | | |
| striped | | | | |
| green | | | | |
| other | | | | |

## What You Need:

**Reproducible** on page 82 for each student

**For each student:** pencil and paper

## What You Do:

**1.** Draw a table on the chalkboard titled "What Students In This Class Are Wearing" with the following categories across: T-shirts, button shirts, pullovers, other; down: blue, red, striped, green, other. (You can "customize" the table according to your students' current fashion statements!) Ask the class how they might fill in the table. (You have to count the number of students in the class that fall into each category.) Look around the class and say, "I see ___ students wearing blue T-shirts. Where does that number go on the table?" Have a volunteer come to the front of the room, write the number in the correct space, and explain why it goes there. Complete the table with other volunteers making observations.

**2.** Make a new table on the chalkboard about the style and color of shoes students wear. Organize the class into pairs and ask each pair to complete a specific section of the table. They should survey the entire class as to footwear and write the results on the board.

**3.** Distribute the **reproducible** on page 82. Read the directions aloud before students complete the sheets on their own.

Answers for page 82: 1. 3; 2. 2; 3. 3; 4. 6; 5. 7

Name_____Date_____

# Used Carriage Lot

This table shows how many different carriages there are in the Used Carriage Lot.

| Model | with horn | padded seats | spare wheel | whip holder | power steering |
|---|---|---|---|---|---|
| One Horse | 4 | 6 | 3 | 1 | 2 |
| Two Horse | 3 | 2 | 6 | 5 | 4 |
| Four Horse | 5 | 3 | 4 | 3 | 5 |
| Six Horse | 7 | 5 | 6 | 4 | 7 |

**1.** How many Four Horse models have whip holders?_____

**2.** How many One Horse models have power steering?_____

**3.** How many Four Horse models have padded seats?_____

**4.** How many Two Horse models have spare wheels?_____

**5.** How many Six Horse models have a horn?_____

Answers on page 81

# It's on the Line

**Objective:** Reading and making line graphs

## What You Need:

**Reproducibles** on pages 84 and 85 for each student

**For each student:** pencil, ruler, sheet of grid paper

**For sharing:** scissors; outdoor thermometer; timer

## What You Do:

**1.** Draw a simple bar graph on the chalkboard, perhaps one about the cost of lunch over a one-week period. (It can be entirely fictional.) Then draw a line graph (using the same scale) that shows the same information. Ask someone to explain how the graphs are similar and how they are different. (They show the same information; one uses a bar, one uses a line.) What would happen if you could put one graph on top of the other? (The dots on the line graph would come to the tops of the bars on the other graphs.)

**2.** To prove this, distribute a sheet of grid paper to students. Ask them to use one half to copy the bar graph and the other half to copy the line graph. Then they can cut the halves apart, place the graphs on top of each other, and hold the papers up to the light to see what happens.

**3.** Distribute the **reproducible** on page 84 to each student. Read the directions aloud and explain how to read the graph before students complete the sheets on their own.

**4.** Place a large, easily readable outdoor thermometer outside a classroom window. Distribute the **reproducible** on page 85 to each student. Read the directions as a class, then help the students decide on a scale for their graphs. Set a timer to ring at hourly intervals so students can read the thermometer and fill out their graphs. Compare graphs at the end of the day.

Answers for page 84: 1. 325°; 2. 250°; 3. 250°; 4. 350°; 5. 150°; 6. 300°

Name_____ Date_____

# Boy, Is It Hot!

Read the graph.  Then answer the questions.

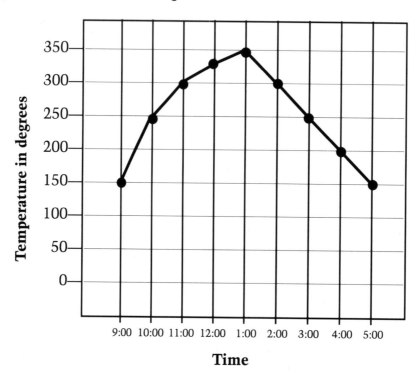

**Temperature on Planet Yamplox**

**1.** What was the temperature at 12:00? _____

**2.** What was the temperature at 3:00? _____

**3.** What was the temperature at 10:00? _____

**4.** What was the temperature at 1:00? _____

**5.** What was the temperature at 9:00? _____

**6.** What was the temperature at 2:00? _____

Answers on page 83

Name_____ Date _____

# Hot or Cold?

Read the thermometer outside the classroom window.  Record the temperature every hour on this graph.

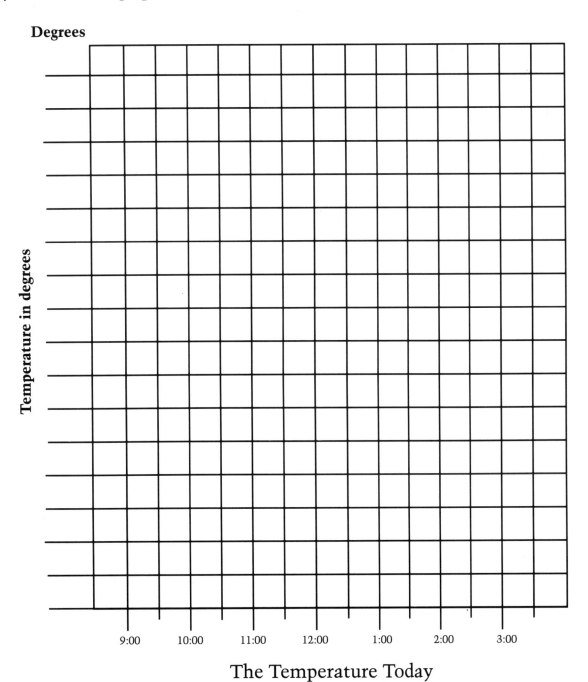

**Degrees**

**Temperature in degrees**

9:00    10:00    11:00    12:00    1:00    2:00    3:00

The Temperature Today

# Circle Around

**Objective: Reading and making circle graphs**

## What You Need:

**Reproducibles** on pages 87 and 88

**For each student:** pencil and paper

**For sharing:** newspapers and magazines

## What You Do:

**1.** Review the concept of percent with the class. Write the percent symbol (%) on the chalkboard. Remind everyone that percent means "part of one hundred." Explain that percentages are portions of real or imagined quantities of one hundred. Ask students to look through old magazines and newspapers to find examples of how percent is used in the real world.

**2.** Draw a large circle on the chalkboard. Explain that a circle graph uses percents, too. Say, "Imagine a pie being divided up for one hundred people." Draw small marks around the edge of the circle. (These need not be perfect hundredths, nor do they need to be all the way around; just enough to give students the idea.) "We can say that one person ate forty of the little pie pieces, or 40% of the pie." Draw lines to show about 40% of the circle. "What part is left?" Children should recognize that the other piece shows 60% of the pie. Repeat this activity, using other numbers and percents suggested by the class.

**3.** Distribute the **reproducible** on page 87 to each student. Read the directions and the title of the graph together. Then give students ample time to work through the pages on their own. Pairs of children can compare answers to check their work.

**4.** Distribute the **reproducible** on page 88. Read the directions aloud before students complete the sheets on their own.

Answers for page 87: 1. 24%; 2. 27%; 3. 10%; 4. 15%; 5. 11%; 6. 13%
Answer for page 88: 4% left over. Count tick marks on graph to determine answer (1 tick mark = 1%). Students can also add up given percents, which add up to 96, and subtract from 100.

Name_____Date _____

# Buford's Bugs

Buford collects bugs. This graph shows what percentage of his collection each kind of bug represents. Read the graph and answer the questions below.

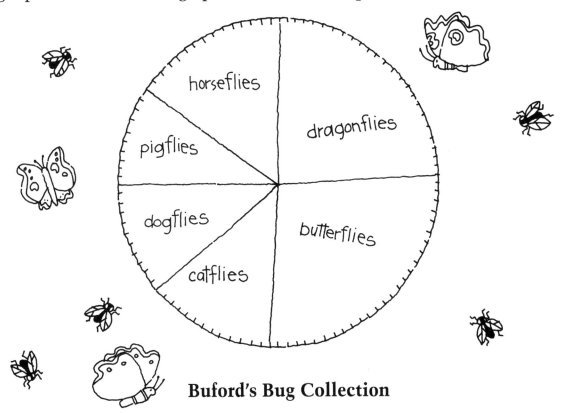

**Buford's Bug Collection**

**1.** What percent of Buford's collection are dragonflies? _____

**2.** What percent of Buford's collection are butterflies? _____

**3.** What percent of Buford's collection are pigflies? _____

**4.** What percent of Buford's collection are horseflies? _____

**5.** What percent of Buford's collection are dogflies? _____

**6.** What percent of Buford's collection are catflies? _____

Answers on page 86

Name_____Date_____

# The Giant Strawberry

Make a graph to show how the giant strawberry was used.

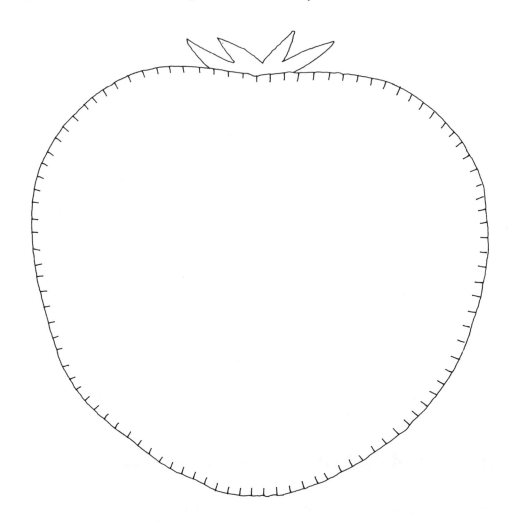

26% was used for pies        15% was used for jam

12% was used for jelly       16% was used for cobbler

9% was used for juice        18% was used for muffins

How much was left over? _____

Answer on page 86

# Use Your Noodle

**Objective: Using logic to solve problems**

## What You Need:

**Reproducible** on page 90 for each student

**For each student:** pencil and paper

**For sharing:** ten to twenty buttons

## What You Do:

**1.** Draw two cars on the chalkboard. As you point to one car, say, "If I told you that these two cars had a race and this one lost, what could you tell me about the other one?" Students should be able to deduce that the other car won the race. Now say, "If I told you that it is snowing outside, what could you tell me about the weather?" Everyone should deduce that it is cold outside. Explain that problems like these are solved by using logic: reasonable, orderly thinking.

**2.** Play a game of "I Spy" with the class. You say, "I spy something in the room. It is square. It is brown. It is not big." Students take turns guessing what it might be. After the first guess, ask, "Why didn't you guess the ___?" The student who answered could explain, for example, "Because it is blue, and you said that the object you spied was brown." Continue to ask the students to justify their guesses. After five unsuccessful guesses, give one more clue. Allow students to take turns giving clues and having the rest of the class guess what they spy.

**3.** Play an elimination game. Place nine buttons on the table in rows of three by three. Mentally select one button and then give clues as to where it is *not*—e.g., "It is not in the third row." Ask someone to take away all the buttons in the third row. "It is not in the second column." Ask a student to remove the buttons in the second column. Continue until only one button is left. As the students catch on to the game, stop removing buttons. Ask them to keep mental track of where the button is not. The first student to correctly guess the secret button can pick the next secret button and give the next set of clues.

**4.** Distribute the **reproducible** on page 90 to each student. Read the directions aloud before students complete the sheets individually. When everyone is finished, ask volunteers to explain how they arrived at their answers.

Answers to page 90: Glup, Plup, Flup, from left to right; Poof, Loof, Foof, Goof, from left to right

Name_____ Date_____

# Clever Caves

Read the clues.  Label the caves where each caveman lives.

Glup does not live next to Flup.
Flup lives in the cave on the right.
Plup lives next to both Glup and Flup.

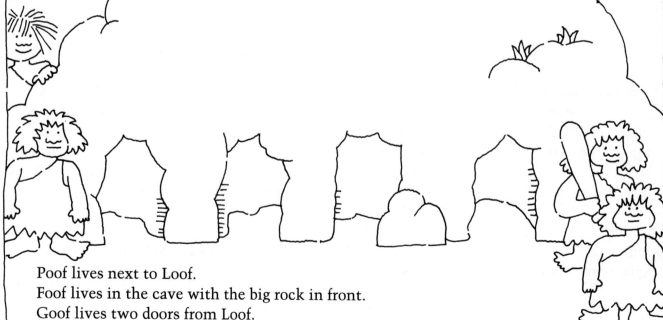

Poof lives next to Loof.
Foof lives in the cave with the big rock in front.
Goof lives two doors from Loof.

Answers on page 89

# Starting at the End

**Objective: Working backwards to solve problems**

## What You Need:

**Reproducible** on page 92 for each student

**For each student:** pencil and paper

**For sharing:** calculators

## What You Do:

**1.** Write these problems on the chalkboard:

___ + 3 = 9

___ - 3 = 9

___ x 3 = 9

___ ÷ 3 = 9

Ask a volunteer to come to the front of the room and find the missing number in the first problem (6). Ask what operation was used to find the answer (subtraction) and write it under the problem. Repeat this routine for the next three problems. Ask if students can see a pattern in the original operation of the problem and the operation that was used to solve the problem. (They are opposites: the addition problem required subtraction; the subtraction problem required addition; the multiplication problem required division; the division problem required multiplication.) Usually we take the original numbers and find an answer. These problems already have answers, and we must find the original numbers used. We call this "working backwards."

**2.** Organize the class into groups of three to four students. Ask each group to write down at least ten problems whose answers are all "12." Have the groups compare their problems. Which were the same? Which were different?

**3.** Distribute the **reproducible** on page 92 to each student. Read the directions aloud before students complete the sheets individually. Allow the use of calculators to complete the page.

**4.** Ask pairs of students to make up three problems that require working backwards to solve. All the problems should be about Pokey's Pet Pigs. Later, the children can exchange problems and solve them.

Answers for page 92: 1. 1,480; 2. 1,582; 3. 1,167; 4. 1,536; 5. 1,928

Name_____ Date_____

# The Princess's Jewels

Princess Gaudyrocks has so many
jewels that she has a hard time keeping
track of them.  Help the Princess's maid
clean up the royal jewelry box.

**1.** The maid found 4,382 diamonds.  She knew she found 1,265 of them under the royal
bed and 1,637 in the royal bathroom.  How many did she find in the royal jewelry box?

_____

**2.** The maid finally found all 3,957 emeralds.  She found 2,007 in the royal wastebasket
and 368 in the royal dresser.  How many emeralds did she find in the royal jewelry
box?_____

**3.** The maid found a total of 6,184 rubies.  She found 2,386 in the royal coffee cup
and 2,631 in the royal teapot.  How many rubies did she find in the royal jewelry
box?_____

**4.** The maid found a total of 5,307 sapphires.  She found 1,768 in the royal closet and
2,003 in the royal bathtub.  How many sapphires did she find in the royal jewelry
box?_____

**5.** The maid found a total of 7,284 opals.  She found 3,196 in the royal slippers, 1,538 in
the royal stereo, and 622 in the royal chamber pot. How many opals did she find in the
royal jewelry box?_____

Answers on page 91

# Step Right Up

**Objective: Solving multiple-step problems**

## What You Need:

**Reproducible** on page 94 for each student

**For each student:** pencil and paper

**For sharing:** calculators

## What You Do:

**1.** Give students a complex, but tasty problem, such as, "I know that doughnuts come in boxes of 12 for $1.32. We have 24 people who will each eat 2 doughnuts. How much should each person contribute to buy the doughnuts?" Ask students what operation they would use to solve this problem. Some may answer, "Multiplication," while others answer, "Division." Point out that they are both correct. They need multiplication and division to solve the problem. First, they need to find the total number of doughnuts needed. (24 people times 2 doughnuts each equals 48 doughnuts needed.) Then they have to find how many boxes of doughnuts they need. (48 doughnuts divided by 12 doughnuts per box equals 4 boxes.) Then they need to know the price of 4 boxes of doughnuts. (4 times $1.32 equals $5.28.) Finally they can divide the total price by the number of people to find what each person should contribute. ($5.28 divided by 24 people equals 22¢ per person.)

**2.** Organize students into pairs. Ask each pair of students to make up two multiple-step problems that involve sums of money. Pairs can trade and solve each other's problems. Ask that they show the steps clearly on their papers. Allow the use of calculators.

**3.** Have the whole class make up a monster multiple-step problem. Begin by setting up the problem. For example, "I went to a restaurant the other day." Act as secretary and record all the conditions of the problem on the chalkboard. Ask children to add sentences to the problem until you think it's complex enough. Then challenge pairs of students to solve the problem.

**4.** Distribute the **reproducible** on page 94 to each student. Read the directions aloud before students complete the sheets on their own. Share answers as a class.

Answers for page 94: 1. $12,107.58; 2. $11,764.44; 3. $12,312.71; 4. $12,753.88

Name_____Date_____

# Custom-Made Motorcycles

The chart shows all the accessories you can get on a new motorcycle. Find out how much each person's motorcycle cost.

| | |
|---|---|
| Hot Shot Motorcycle..................$9,375.00 | |
| Aooga horn ..............................$187.46 | Saddle bags ..............$596.00 |
| Fake fur seats .........................$754.98 | Brakes.....................$691.64 |
| Side car..................................$3,734.62 | Leather jacket .........$512.53 |
| Big engine ...............................$1,472.77 | Cool sunglasses ........$139.42 |
| Really big engine ......................$5,832.57 | |

**1.** Spiker bought a Hot Shot with fake fur seats and a really big engine. The dealer gave him $3,854.97 off the price for his trade-in. What did he pay for his Hot Shot?_____

**2.** Zebra bought a Hot Shot with a side car, big engine, and cool sunglasses. The dealer gave Zebra $2,957.37 for her trade-in. How much did she pay for her Hot Shot?_____

**3.** Moose bought a Hot Shot with an aooga horn, brakes, a really big engine, and a leather jacket. The dealer gave him $4,286.49 for his trade-in. How much did he pay for his Hot Shot?_____

**4.** Tigra bought a Hot Shot with saddle bags, cool sunglasses, a big engine, fake fur seats, and brakes. The dealer gave her $275.93 for her trade-in. How much did Tigra pay for her Hot Shot?_____

Answers on page 93

# Tell Me More

**Objective: Solving problems with too much or too little information**

## What You Need:

**Reproducible** on page 96 for each student

**For each student:** pencil and paper

**For sharing:** calculators

## What You Do:

**1.** Write a problem such as, "The ruler costs 25¢ more than the pencil. How much do they cost together?" and ask students for the answer. They should tell you that they can't find the answer. Ask them to explain why. (There is too little information.) Ask what they need to know to find the answer. (Either the price of the pencil or the price of the ruler.) Write another problem such as, "Mary is 60 inches tall. Fred is 63 inches tall. Arthur is 62 inches tall. Martha is 57 inches tall. How much taller than Mary is Fred?" Ask the class what is wrong with this problem. (There is too much information, so it is difficult to figure out which is needed information.)

**2.** Organize students into pairs and ask the partners to write one problem that has too little information and one problem that has too much information. All the problems should be about Henrietta's Happy Hogs. The pairs can exchange papers and identify the problem with too little information and solve the problem with too much information.

**3.** Distribute the **reproducible** on page 96 to each student. Read the directions aloud before students complete the sheets individually. Ask students to make up any information that was missing in the problems on this reproducible that had too little information. They can then solve those problems, too.

Answers for page 96: 1. too little;  2. too much—61 pounds;  3. too little;  4. too much—$12,517.96;  5. too much—$3,671.60

Name_____ Date_____

# Carnival Time!

Read the problems.  Mark each problem as having too much or too little information.  Solve the problem if you can.

**1.** The circus trailer weighs 746 pounds more than the elephant.  How much does the elephant weigh?

[ ] too much
[ ] too little
_____

**2.** The strong man can lift 356 pounds.  The bearded lady can lift 125 pounds.  The clown's real name is Murray.  The tall man can lift 64 pounds.  How much more can the bearded lady lift than the tall man?

[ ] too much
[ ] too little
_____

**3.** The fire-eater eats corn flakes for breakfast.  How much does the midget weigh?

[ ] too much
[ ] too little
_____

**4.** The afternoon performance made $5,253.90.  The snake charmer's brother sell cars.  The night performance made $7,264.06.  How much did the carnival make today?

[ ] too much
[ ] too little
_____

**5.** The half-man half-woman shaves both sides of his/her face.  The ringmaster earns $367.16 every performance.  The lion tamer feeds his lions 268 steaks every day.  How much does the ringmaster earn for 10 performances a week?

[ ] too much
[ ] too little
_____

Answers on page 95

**96**